Creating a Learning School

Creating a Learning School

David Middlewood,
Richard Parker &
Jackie Beere

Paul Chapman Publishing

© 2005 David Middlewood,Richard Parker and Jackie Beere

First published 2005

Paul Chapman Publishing
A SAGE Publications Company
1 Oliver's Yard
55 City Road
London EC1Y 1SP

SAGE Publications Inc
2455 Teller Road
Thousand Oaks, California 91320

SAGE Publications India Pvt Ltd
B-42, Panchsheel Enclave
Post Box 4109
New Delhi 110 017

Library of Congress Control Number: 2004116160

A catalogue record for this book is available from the British
Library

ISBN 1-4129-1041-2
ISBN 1-4129-1042-0 (pbk)

Typeset by GCS, Leighton Buzzard, Beds.
Printed in Great Britain by Athenaeum Press Ltd., Gateshead

CONTENTS

FIGURES

About the Authors

DAVID MIDDLEWOOD was until recently deputy director of the Centre for Educational Leadership and Management of the University of Leicester, where he worked for fourteen years. Previously he was a headteacher of a secondary comprehensive school for ten years, following a career in schools and colleges since the 1960s. He is currently a Research Associate of the University of Lincoln, and an occasional lecturer in educational leadership and management at De Montfort University.

David has lectured and researched in New Zealand and in South Africa, where he has been a visiting professor and also studied schools in Greece and Australia. He has devised and contributed to training programmes for school leaders from China and Indonesia.

David has published widely, on strategic management, curriculum management, home–school links and especially on a whole range of human resource issues such as appraisal, recruitment and selection, induction, staff development and motivation. His books include *Leading and Managing People in Education* (with Tony Bush) – second edition 2005, *Managing Teacher Appraisal and Performance: a comparative approach* with Carol Cardno (2001), and *Practitioner Research in Education* (1999). He has co-edited and contributed chapters to various edited volumes, including the Commonwealth Secretariat series of books on educational management in South Africa. David has recently been involved in research on teaching assistants, induction for new headteachers, senior leadership teams, schools under threat, and inclusive schools. David was co-editor of the UK publications, *Headship Matters* and *Primary Headship* from 1999–2005.

RICHARD PARKER is currently principal of Beauchamp College in Oadby, Leicestershire, a 14–18 school with one of the largest post-16 cohorts in the country. It is a specialist college with training school status. Previously Richard was head of a comprehensive school in Corby for ten years helping transform it into one of the best performing schools, as well as obtaining his own Masters degree. He had taught for twenty years before that in schools in the South.

Richard has been involved at national level with specialist schools and is a member of a government advisory group at present. He is a tutor for Leicester University and co-authored a chapter on support staff in *Managing the Curriculum* (2001 Paul Chapman), as well as being co-editor of *Headship Matters* 1999–2005. He carried out research for the National College for School

Leadership on leaders' life histories. He is particularly committed in his practice to extended schooling in which Beauchamp is a leading national institution.

JACKIE BEERE is headteacher of Campion School in Northamptonshire, UK, where she was previously deputy head. After years of teaching, she became one of the first Advanced Skills Teachers and is now a regular speaker and presenter on creative learning. She and her school are members of the Campaign for Learning and she was awarded the OBE for services to education.

Jackie is a university tutor and has been responsible for establishing a Masters course at her own school, having first obtained her own MBA. She published a successful book on teaching strategies at Key Stage Three. She was invited to join the Government's think tank on developing personalised learning as one of the most successful practitioners in the field. The resultant paper (2005) 'About Learning' helped Jackie's ideas develop, sometimes beyond those expressed in this book.

Preface

The main impetus for the writing of this book comes from the fact that we are all passionately committed to a move away from the obsession with education being perceived as merely a means to an end and schools valued according to their test and examination results. We, like many others in education, have a huge desire to see learning as central to the process of schooling. As mature adults, we have become more not less excited by our own learning as time passes and have often felt keenly the sense of waste when we hear young people speak of their schooling as boring and who are impatient for it to finish. The fault in most case is not theirs.

Although we have ideals, we are also pragmatists who believe that for the people in our schools the future starts – now. Actions have to be taken and taken soon. The case studies in this book show just how many of our schools share such beliefs and are already doing things to make their students' and staff's experiences meaningful, relevant and exciting. There are also many schools where people would like to make changes but are not sure how to begin or lack confidence to do so. There are also schools where initiatives have been begun, only for them to founder after a while, causing a loss of faith in the change process itself.

This book attempts to take a whole school view of approaches to making learning central, so that staffing and structures, external links and resources, are all dealt with in examining ways in which learning schools can evolve. We believe that unless every aspect of a school's life is put under scrutiny, an emphasis on learning will remain an 'add on'. This of course does not mean everything can be attempted at once! School leaders and managers are astute people and know that what you do next depends on what you are doing now. Nearly all the chapters therefore include suggestions for practical and specific steps that you may wish to consider as the next step for your school. We have set out a model for change within which these steps can be taken.

Because of the uniqueness of individual learners and of individual schools, no book can provide the answers. Rather, we have sought to provide the opportunity for the right questions to be asked. We do not underestimate the huge difficulties faced by schools in some particular circumstances but are also clear that doing nothing and staying the same is not an option.

The first two chapters set out our vision of what a learning school will look like and why such schools are so needed. Each of Chapters 3 to 11 examines a particular aspect of schools: leadership, staffing, classroom practice, assessment, curriculum extra, resourcing, the parents' role. Chapter 9 attempts to offer a view of learning during schooling years as a journey of constant transitions, whilst the final chapter takes an overview of what all the aspects covered mean for the future of schooling and beyond, including their impact on all those involved with schools. We should also say that, all three of us share the same purpose and philosophy which shape this book, the responsibility for the specific ideas and suggestions for action in individual chapters are primarily those of the author or authors of those chapters.

Our beliefs come from the extensive experience of teaching as well as leadership and management that we have all had. One of us was a headteacher for ten years and has since taught and researched in higher education for over a decade; the second is currently in his second headship, after ten years in his first, and the third has relatively recently taken up her first headship. Our focus is on the secondary years of schooling, because this is where our experience mainly lies, but we are acutely conscious that, for the learning schools ideal to be fully accomplished, the early and primary years remain fundamental.

It is hoped that this book will encourage and inspire those who are also committed to the love of learning to try new ideas which will help others to share that love. We quickly realised in setting out to write the book that there was much more to leave out than it was possible to put in. We are aware of how much more could be said on each topic but believe that what is included will give food for thought and also action. Our grateful thanks go to Tracy Harazdiuk for all her early work on the manuscript, to Felicity Murray for her invaluable work in preparing the book for publication, and to Jacqui, Nora, and John respectively for their help and support to us throughout this project. Finally, we express our appreciation to all the students, teachers and staff with whom we have worked, exchanged ideas, and who have inspired us to believe that such schools as envisaged here are possible. More research continues to be needed and we hope that schools will wish to be involved in this.

David Middlewood
Richard Parker
Jackie Beere

Chapter 1

What Will Learning Schools Look Like?

Preview

In the context of describing the key features of a learning school, this chapter considers the following questions:

- What will its ethos and culture be like?
- What will relationships be like?
- What kind of organisational structures will it have?
- How will it display its accountability?

Chapter 1 also offers some initial thoughts about managing change.

> *I'd like a school that I'd get up in the morning and say, 'Great, it's school and I'm going to learn lots! Then when I got home, I'd just want the next day to come.'*
>
> 13 year-old pupil

Ethos and culture

The general 'feel' of a school which has learning at its centre will involve certain beliefs and values which are held by everyone, which will influence the recruitment and appointment of new employees, and are the embodiment in action to which everyone is committed. These include:

- a belief that learning is a lifelong process towards which schools contribute;
- a belief that effort can lead to success;
- a belief that everyone has the capacity to learn and improve;
- a belief that challenging situations, problems and tasks are preferable to easy ones;
- a belief in teamwork;
- a belief that understanding of the whole person is crucial to facilitating their ability to learn;
- a recognition that schools are the hub of an extended local community and that engaging parents, school neighbours and community members in its processes is central to its existence.

Without such beliefs being held by the people who work in the school, the students, parents and others connected with it cannot be expected to be convinced that theirs is a place where learning really does matter as the most important reason for everyone being there. However, this convincing will only occur through the *experience* of the children, pupils and students, not through brochures, open evenings or speeches. Our own extensive experience of working with and talking with youngsters in and out of school suggests that their experience of school should include:

- being praised for their successes and having these celebrated;
- being challenged if they are not putting sufficient effort into their learning;
- being shown that when they get something wrong, it becomes a chance to learn how and why;
- being recognised as an individual;
- being helped to discover what are their individual most effective ways of learning and to assess their own development, progress and achievement;
- having the opportunity to make a difference to the way the school operates;
- having the opportunity to work and learn with people younger and older than themselves, as well as their peers;
- building on what they have already learned and link with what they learn outside of school;
- feeling safe and secure, both physically and mentally, in the school environment;
- and having what they learn and achieve recognised beyond school, in further and higher education, by employers and the world of work generally.

Relationships

One of the most striking aspects of the learning school and one that it is hoped would be clear to anyone visiting the school would be the nature of the relationships between the various people who are engaged in the school's activities. Schools, like most organisations, have a complex web of relationships at their heart, but they are quite unlike commercial organisations in that this complexity is compounded by the fact that relationships over which the school has little influence impinge directly on the main client's (the pupil/student) activity, i.e. learning.

However collaborative a school is, each person has his or her own world at their centre as a starting point and each different person sees the other person as being part of their world. The analogy with a traditional family may be apt. Imagine a grandmother and grandfather with, say, four adult children (two sons, two daughters), each of whom has two children. They will see themselves and their family relationships as precisely that: 'We have four children and eight grandchildren'.

2

The eldest son will see *his* family as the centre: 'I and my partner have two children. I have two parents who are my children's grandparents, as are my partner's parents. I also have one brother and two sisters.' The son's world involves relationships not necessarily related to his parents and his relationships with his brother and sisters are of quite a different nature from that of his parents. And so on.

Although all this may be obvious, some of the literature on schools appears to take individuals' willingness to collaborate in powerful professional relationships for granted, whereas to ignore human beings' instinct to see themselves as the starting point may be foolish. The relationships within a school may be more like a vast honeycomb of interlocking and overlapping relationships and the challenge facing those developing learning is to work at discovering and developing what holds the whole thing together.

Whose relationships?

To represent the 'role set' of even one person, the pupil or student learner, shows the range of relationships in one person's world (see Figure 1.1).

Figure 1.1 *Role set of a pupil or student learner.*

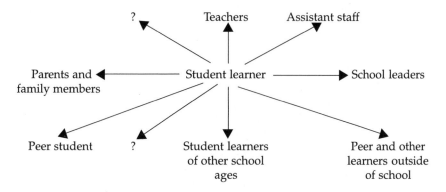

No doubt there are others that can be supplied for individuals, and of course each of the above can be sub-divided e.g. into boys and girls and peer groups.

A further point to make is that these relationships are bounded by the specific learning context. Thus in the conventional classroom, the immediate relationships are between:

- teacher;
- student;
- other students in the class;
- assistant staff (as in Figure 1.2).

Whereas in the corridors and during breaks between lessons, they will be quite different, as they will at home.

3

Figure 1.2 *Classroom relationships.*

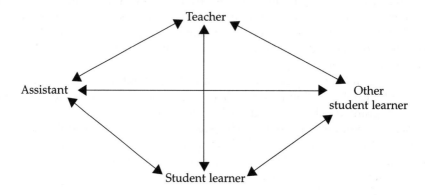

Similarly for staff of a school, quite different role sets exist for some of the time, involving for example colleagues and school-leaders. Yet it is in the specific learning context that parallels appear, thus underpinning the point that the focus on learning and the willingness of all at the school to see learning as their starting point can be the key to these relationships.

The challenge therefore for the learning school is how to support the focus on the needs and development of the individual learner, whilst supporting teams, groups, partnerships and the whole organisation. (Staff relationships are discussed in Chapter 4.) A crucial example will be the organisation of learning groups. These will be based on learning needs and since these needs vary, groupings will vary, instead of being fixed by ability or gender. A 13 year-old, for example, may sometimes be in a group with other 13 year-olds, sometimes in a group with other students across a wide age range of school age students, sometimes in one with 13 or 14 year-olds, sometimes in a single sex group, sometimes in a group with part-time adult learners, sometimes in a group with common learning styles.

The flexibility in group composition is crucial in addressing learning needs because the consistency exists in the focus on learning. Moreover, although more complex organisationally, the task of the teacher is actually easier in each of the specific groups above because of the commonality of the learners involved.

Of course, for children and young people, the socialisation aspect of schooling remains important, and the adolescent, for example, is likely to need the security of one group with whom he or she meets regularly and can readily share personal issues such as – what it is like to *be* a 14 year-old boy or girl? Hence, the need for the equivalent of a tutor group (discussed in Chapter 4).

Partnerships for learning

If every relationship in this honeycomb can be viewed, aspirationally at least, as a partnership for learning, we should reflect on what most of us consider constitutes an effective partnership.

4

Our discussions with teachers on this topic have led us to believe these include:

- a clear purpose – agreed by the partners;
- recognition of the complementary roles of those involved;
- good communication between them (including listening);
- regular monitoring of how the partnership is working;
- a commitment to continually improve;
- a need for mutual trust and respect.

The aspiration, therefore, is for the acknowledgement of 'We're in this together' as being the approach underpinning how relationships in the learning school are expressed. How might it show itself to the visitor, mentioned at the start of this section? In language, behaviour and in the use of and attitude to authority.

Language

Research, such as that of Lodge (2003), shows that *talking* about learning not only helps make learning the focus of attention but that it helps young people practise and develop a language relating to that learning.

> *Children wanted to talk about it (learning). As a result of increased talk about learning young people have become more effective learners and often improve academically.*

> (Lodge, 2003 p.7)

Similarly with school staff, Carnell (2001) found that staff learning was developed through dialogue – the more people discovered about their learning, the more they wanted to talk about it, and the more they talked about it, the more they wanted to find out.

The involvement in regular talk helps the school inhabitants and stakeholders develop a common language and this aids understanding. For example, understanding the difference between 'discussion' and 'dialogue'. Senge (1990) describes discussion as being where each person brings their own point of view and argues for it, whereas dialogue is where everyone suspends assumptions and genuinely thinks together. He suggests that everyone in a dialogue should see each other as 'colleagues'. In a school, this would cover not only when staff meet together but also when teachers and students or any other partners talk – they are all colleagues in learning, a context that sits easily with the concept of teacher as learner.

Precise common meanings develop so that 'reflection' does not mean, in a loose way, 'just thinking about', but asking oneself specific questions about what has occurred.

In a learning school, the daily language reflects the approach to issues that arise in the school. The use of 'we' and 'our' rather than 'I' and 'my' pre-dominates. A problem, for example, is *our* problem rather than *my* problem (except when intensely personal). This is not idealistic, because the competition between departments in terms of results that currently exists in many secondary schools ('Why does that department let the rest of us down with its weak results?') has no place in a school where student learning is central. 'Why are our students achieving less in some areas than others?' becomes a question for all staff.

Behaviour

A number of the issues referred to here will be returned to in later chapters because the behaviour of the school's inhabitants is greatly influenced by factors such as environment, staffing and community engagement. Egan (1982) described two of the key ingredients in supportive behaviour as:

- *confidentiality* – 'if I tell this person about myself, she will not tell others.'

This sits perfectly comfortably with an ethos of openness and trust, where information is shared and there are few secrets. And:

- *credibility* – 'an expectancy held by every individual or group that the word, promise, verbal or written statement of another individual or group can be relied on.'

There can be no favouritism, since all are respected as individual learners. If, for example, my favoured learning style is auditory, I do not favour other auditory learners above visual or kinaesthetic learners. I may have more empathy with auditory learners but I respect – and perhaps secretly envy! – others as different but equally effective learners.

It is relatively easy to give a list of attributes of people's behaviour that are desirable e.g:

- using humour;
- being willing to apologise;
- being ready to admit ignorance;

but people only develop patterns of behaviour if they are visible and audible on a daily basis, and Bentley (1998) suggests that 'mutuality' is the key to learning relationships. One teacher for a higher degree assignment researched students' perceptions of an effective teacher. High on the list of students' 'pet hates' was:

Teachers who expect you to laugh at their jokes but can't take one themselves!

Equally important is that behaviour ensures the feelings of safety and security essential to emotional wellbeing and learning referred to earlier. The traditional organisation of schools has unfortunately meant that in some children have felt vulnerable and threatened, at their worst reflecting and reinforcing some of society's worst traits through what Harber (2004) has seen as their militaristic rituals and traditions. Only a rose-tinted view of human nature would envisage these traits disappearing but a focus on individual and collective learning helps over a period of time to develop more of the trust and respect necessary to mitigate the worst of their effects. Some of the ways in which staff can help in this are addressed in Chapter 4.

Use of and attitude to authority

Bentley (1998) suggests that the power relationship between teacher and student will shift at times. Sometimes the student will be the lead learner, sometimes, the teacher. However, within the context of the partnerships we are suggesting, this is less of a risk than might appear.

However, in all descriptions of 'student-centred' schools with mutual learning, it is important not to forget the most obvious fact that staff are adults, students are children or young people. Moreover staff are paid employees, students attend because the law requires them to do so, however willingly we hope they do so. Adult staff have:

- training;
- specialist expertise;
- mostly self-sufficient lives outside of school;
- a more 'established' character and personality;
- experience – of life, adult relationships, employment, etc.

An intense focus on learning in no way diminishes the adults; rather it provides greater challenges for them in the work and in their role as learner and teacher. The scope for misuse of power/authority in the school and classroom has always been considerable and the history of education has too many examples, but in a learning context where there are, say, two adults and 24 students, the adults need to be viewed as 'authoritative'. To be an authority on history, or literature, or physics or learning is quite different from exercising authority as power. In a learning school, the member of staff is perceived as having authority and as being the kind of person who will not misuse it.

This authority sits, as all relationships do, within certain structures.

Structures

Structures and organisation of staffing, curriculum, the school hours etc are dealt with in Chapter 4. Here, we are concerned with the ways in which the leadership, management and organisation of the school can foster and facilitate the development of relationships as envisaged above. Such structures will need to facilitate, for example:

- time for staff to meet and talk;

- easy and effective communication both by voice and e-mail but also through physical proximity of staff in the same teams;
- ability and autonomy to create learning teams;
- opportunities for informal one-to-one and also group dialogues;
- development of structured opportunities for the student voice, such as councils or circle time (for too long wrongly associated only with primary schools);
- opportunities for pupil shadowing, staff shadowing, etc;
- ways in which meaningful ritual and ceremony can be enacted.

(Adapted from Carnell and Lodge, 2002)

Structures give frameworks – which are appreciated by all people, and especially young people – within which individuals, groups and teams can operate in a climate of agreed values, working for an agreed purpose. In the learning school, for example, all individuals whether adult or student should be respected for wanting to work on their own if need be, but no one should feel isolated. Additionally, the structures need to allow what is seen currently as a luxury, namely non-activity. Learning schools will be busy, active places but all learning experiences show the value of occasionally 'doing nothing'!

The issue of staff working groups and staff meetings can be taken as illustrative. As far as I am concerned, the learning school when fully established will have no compulsory meetings. It may be necessary, as some schools have already done, to reduce gradually the number of meetings in order to achieve this, but the quality of meetings timetabled regularly for a post-school slot is generally deemed to be poor. The starting point is, as always, purpose:

- Why are we meeting?
- If there appears to be a need for a meeting, can the apparent purpose (e.g. sharing information, receiving comment) be done in another way?
- Is all the meeting relevant to all the people there?
- Most importantly, have we reviewed how good/useful the meeting was?

In the learning school, there will be many occasions when people wish to meet and the key word here is *wish*. Thus:

- all meetings will be voluntary;
- all will take the form of a dialogue, led by a facilitator.

In the learning school, the voluntary meetings may, on some occasions, go further and adopt the strategy of some business organisations which want to avoid 'group-think' and encourage genuine thinking as well as good use of time by having – **no chairs**!

A large number of people think most effectively when they walk around (at home for example they might be gardening or taking the dog for a walk), so it makes no sense to insist that everyone sits at a table and therefore impose one

Case example

One school in Northamptonshire, England, set about a complete overhaul of its meetings, both in quantity and quality, as a result of concern about ineffective use of staff time. The outcomes of their overhaul were:

(a) A target was set to reduce meetings by 20 per cent over the next year and by a further ten per cent the following year.
(b) Agendas for meetings would include alongside each agenda item the purpose of having it on the agenda, thus reducing frustration of mixed expectations e.g. between decision-making and discussion.
(c) All agendas would be ordered so that any items not relevant to some members would be dealt with first, enabling them to leave early. This was to be evened out over a period so that everyone would at some time leave early!
(d) All sections of the school which called meetings were to devise their own 'golden rules', so that each group had ownership of the way meetings were conducted.

The whole school survey had shown that the commonest complaint of staff about meetings was by far failure to start and finish on time, so how this was to be dealt with was to included in these 'golden rules'. Examples of rules which emerged were:

- No soap-boxing!
- No whingeing!
- No waffling!
- No side-conversations!
- People arriving late to enter quietly, ask no questions and catch up on business after the meeting.
- Three minutes before the scheduled end, a brief review of the meeting as a process is carried out.
- The chairperson must not also be the time-keeper!

learning style on everyone. Walking into a meeting in progress in a learning school, you might see various people standing up, walking round, taking a drink of water, jotting something on a pad or flipchart, talking in twos or threes, talking to themselves. This is simply another example of putting the people first, as in our adult learning lives, rather than saying 'The system is that we all sit down round a table.'

If a specific organisational issue or plan needs to be addressed, working or task groups will:

- be composed of volunteers;
- and a facilitator will be appointed from within the group;
- any groups dealing with ideas for curriculum changes would include involvement of student learning representatives and representatives of parents.

The principles underpinning all structures in the learning school are:

- they are non-hierarchical (because hierarchy fosters dependence);
- they encourage engagement (by people who *choose* to be involved);
- they encourage autonomy in decision-making (as discussed in Chapter 3);
- they remain flexible (to regularly accommodate new developments/ initiatives).

Far from fostering uncertainty, such structures require complete clarity concerning roles (not job descriptions!) and responsibilities. For example, schools continue to operate within statutory frameworks in fields as diverse as curriculum and health and safety. The duty of care for students and staff under the latter heading is crucial and legal requirements with regard to recruitment procedures or staff entitlements must be followed. There is no question of a learning-centred school existing in a vacuum. It needs to be as accountable to those it serves as any other school.

Accountability

Earlier in this chapter it was made clear that it was essential for students, no matter how personally fulfilling they found their experience of school, to have the results of that experience recognised beyond school in terms of their need to go on to employment or further or higher education. This is returned to in later chapters. For this to be ensured, learning schools need to remain open and accountable, not only to their internal stakeholders (students and staff) but to their immediate external ones, such as parents, local communities etc, and to regional and national stakeholders (see Figure 1.3).

This accountability will need to include:

- showing that the school's systems for achieving its goals are appropriate;
- showing that the school is operating in an ethically and legally appropriate manner;
- showing that all members of staff and their performance are being appropriately managed.

The first two of these will cause schools few problems, as the emphasis of the last decades has subjected school systems to intense scrutiny. Indeed, the indications in the UK that there may be a movement towards the more self-evaluative

Figure 1.3 *Accountability framework for the learning school.*

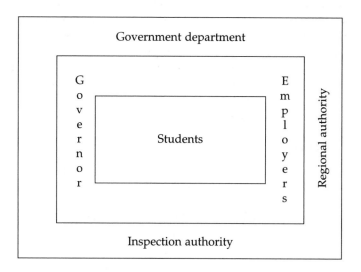

processes of various countries are encouraging in this context. However, the way in which teachers and other members of staff are managed, especially in terms of how their performance is assessed, will need a major overhaul for it to be relevant to the context of a learning school.

Assessing teachers in teaching schools

In the current context of utilitarian processes (discussed in Chapter 2), assessment of teaching performance is inevitably based mainly on measurable pupil outcomes. Research in English schools carried out by one of the authors (Middlewood, 2002) examined discrepancies between gradings of certain teachers by inspectors and the assessment of those same teachers by their headteachers. Inspectors inspect a school over four days – or less time – and individual teachers are seen teaching in their classrooms for one, or up to four occasions. These visits are not necessarily for a whole lesson, and the lessons are graded from excellent to poor. The purpose of the research was to compare the way the assessments were made in order to ascertain which was more likely to be compatible with teacher assessment in the emerging learning context.

All headteachers in the research felt that such discrepancies:

- damaged the credibility of the whole process;
- lowered the self-esteem of other teachers;
- showed the weakness of assessment based on 'one-off' visits which could be prepared for anyway;
- with the appearance of objectivity, the inspectors' judgements were based on a narrow model of teaching and learning.

It should be mentioned that some inspectors' assessments concurred with those of the headteacher. What these discrepancies point to is the risk inherent in operating a system of assessment which is so narrow and outcomes-focused. It is this narrowness and focus on prescribed outcomes that makes it so attractive to those who operate external inspections and produce judgements via a once-only process. The assessments of the headteachers, on the other hand, were based on data gathered over a period of time, a period which will see below par performance by even the best teachers on some days but builds up a cumulative picture of effectiveness, using a variety of data sources.

Assessing teachers in learning schools

Notice that this assessment refers to 'teachers' not just 'teaching'. The reason is very simply that, as anyone doing the job will tell you, there is a lot more than teaching to being a teacher! The multi-tasking of teachers in countries such as the UK is enormous, as described in the Relationships section above. Any assessment of a teacher therefore needs to take account of their overall role in the school, never forgetting that their key role is in the classroom. The outcomes based model of assessment is clearly inadequate but any new model faces certain problems.

If the task of the teacher is to manage learning, with the emphasis therefore on the process of learning, there are a number of difficulties that appear to present themselves:

- If the ultimate progress in learning is *internal* – can it be 'seen'?
- If the teacher's influence is *indirect* – can it be isolated?
- If the teacher provides only *opportunities* for learning, what happens if learners do not take them?

The issue of context should eventually be less important than at present since the focus on learning as a process is predicated upon the assumption that everyone is a learner with a learning potential for life, and whilst context may affect measurable outcomes, it will be less important to the effective teacher. It could even be argued that it will be fairer to effective teachers who work in less supportive physical and socio-economic environments since it will not start with an assumption that students in those circumstances have built-in disadvantages in achieving specific outcomes such as test scores and exam results.

Furthermore, as learning patterns change in the twenty-first century, there will be more learning situations away from the physical presence of the teacher, thus reducing the emphasis on controlled artificial contexts on which assessment is based. This may also lead to more formal recognition of the role played by others (especially parents, perhaps) in the learning process.

Further research carried out with focus groups of teachers in the early years of their career (Middlewood, 2002) found that they:

(a) Were scathing of the current assessment model, some of them believing that it actually penalised good teachers through protecting weak teachers who 'taught to the test'.

(b) Strongly favoured a form of assessment which would:
  i take account of feedback from students, parents and colleagues;
  ii emphasise team assessment rather than individual assessment;
  iii use qualitative data as much as quantitative.

It is not difficult in a learning school where relationships thrive with a climate of trust to devise a model of review of performance for *all* employees which would involve these three elements. Not only would such a model be encouraging individual, team and organisational learning through the feedback generated but it would be demonstrating to those outside that the school is robust as well as reflective, and can submit readily to scrutiny from external frameworks.

Further aspects of accountability are dealt with in Chapters 5 and 9.

Making the change

The final section of this chapter deals with the issue of what is involved in making and managing the change from wherever the individual school is now to becoming a true learning school. This after all is what this book is about and each of Chapters 3 to 11 deals with a specific aspect of the learning school and the changes that may be needed in that area. Learning schools have to be well led of course and Chapter 3 examines the kinds of leaders and leadership that will be needed, whilst Chapters 4 and 5 extend this to staffing, looking at structures and roles as well as staff commitment to their own learning. Chapters 7 and 8 examine student learning, both inside the 'classroom' and the school as a whole, while Chapter 10 confirms the importance of assessment in developing student learning.

Of course, although resources are known to be crucial to the effectiveness of schools, history has shown that it is not as much the quantity of resources as their relevance, appropriateness and flexibility that is crucial, as Chapter 6 discusses. Other resources include those which stakeholders have to offer and Chapter 11 looks at the role of the most important stakeholders – the parents.

Of course, learning schools cannot exist in a vacuum and Chapter 9 looks at effective transitions, the most important examples being from primary to secondary schools and from the end of statutory schooling to full adult life, while recognising that for the young learner all learning takes place during transition of some kind. The final chapter takes an overview of the whole move forward that this book envisages.

First, however, we need to remember that, as Fullan, has said: 'Change is a process, not an event' (Fullan, 2001) – a school does not become a learning school overnight.

Secondly, change will only occur through the mindsets of those people involved being engaged with the ideas within the envisaged change – all those involved with the school (especially the staff) need to *feel* the value of the new things being done – emphasis here is on emotions and values, not rationality and cogent reasoning.

Schools that set out to change may find that:

- they show the slow and bureaucratic change characteristic of prescriptive organisations;
- or they show the rapid intuitive change of entrepreneurial organisations which do not have time to think;
- or they make some changes but lack the continued capacity to change characteristic of unlearning organisations.

(Based on West-Burnham and O'Sullivan, 1998 pp.38–39)

Change in particular practice can be gradual and can take a considerable period to evolve. The tension for schools of course is that

> *while it takes time for teachers to learn and embed new practices, for the pupils it's the only time they have. Their school years are precious ones and can't be repeated.*
> (Stoll et al, 2003 p.19)

It has been argued that there are three cultural change processes based on a continuum from 'evolutionary' through 'addictive' to 'transformational' change:

- *Evolutionary change:* which is implicit, unconscious and unplanned, with norms, values and beliefs fading and appearing over time.
- *Addictive change:* which may or may not be explicit and conscious, since norms, beliefs and values are suddenly modified when new initiatives are introduced.
- *Transformational change:* which gives deliberate attention to changing norms, values and beliefs.

(Based on Rossman et al, 1998)

Which is the appropriate process for 'your' school will depend upon where the school is at this point. What is clear is that all of us concerned with schools have ourselves to learn to change so that we can help students to learn to manage, cope with and thrive during the period of change. This not only ensures their 'precious' years are not put at risk but that they are ready to thrive during a life of continual change.

Sustainability of change

The regular failure of apparently effective changes in educational organisations has led to much debate about the 'sustainability' of change. Hargreaves and Fink

(2000 p.32) make a distinction between 'sustainability' and 'maintainability', suggesting that true change is about much more than how to make change last:

> *It addresses how particular initiatives can be developed without compromising the development of others in the surrounding environment, now and in the future.*

This clearly has an ethical dimension:

- that change that is sustainable contributes to the good of *everyone;*
- others not directly involved do not suffer as a result of an initiative;
- that resources will be sustainable to match the rate of change in the future. These are more likely to be in human resource development rather than capital investment, necessary though this will be.

We believe that the learning school is such an initiative because it invests in learning and is not merely altering schooling.

Specific steps

One of the purposes of this book is to help leaders, managers and staff of schools who wish to make progress towards being a learning school by making practical suggestions of steps they might take. Which steps will depend upon where you feel the school is at the present. The authors of this book are quite clear that, in order to achieve the transformation required, there is a sequence of steps which will bring dividends.

There is already evidence that schools that adopt a new initiative, such as the learning styles of visual, auditory and kinaesthetic (VAK), and apply it to certain classes or groups, are extremely unlikely to become effective learning schools. Such approaches mean that these initiatives remain 'added-on' and do not become embedded in the school's whole approach to learning. Advocates of Accelerated Learning also stress that it is:

> *not about drinking water, eating bananas, listening to Mozart and doing brain breaks ... it is about a ... structured model.*
>
> (Smith et al, 2003)

One of the authors of this book, Jackie Beere, devised a framework (or hierarchy) for development of steps towards the learning school and each of Chapters 3 to 11 uses this framework to put forward practical suggestions for making change. Again, which ones you take depend on what you have already done (see Figure 1.4).

It may be seen as a checklist for development, but a checklist where the changes should be looked at carefully in a specific order. First, what about the learning environment – in the school as a whole, the staff areas, the classroom etc. Are there steps to be taken here? Then – relationships. These have been

Figure 1.4 *Learning to learn – hierarchy of needs (Beere, 2003).*

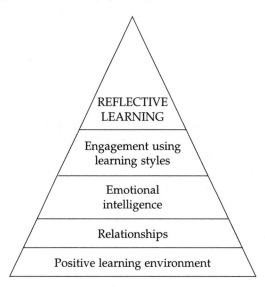

discussed generally in this chapter but what about in specific areas: in the school as a whole, between staff, in the classroom, with parents etc? And so on.

We believe that deliberate steps – *chosen by those who best know the context of the individual school* – are the most likely way in which the transformation into a learning school can be achieved. Chapter 2 considers the reasons why such schools are needed in the twenty-first century.

References

Beere, J. (2003) *Learning to Learn: Hierarchy of Needs.* www.campaign-for-learning.org.uk

Bentley, T. (1998) *Learning Beyond the Classroom: Education for a Changing World.* London: Routledge.

Carnell, E. (2001) 'The value of meta-learning dialogue', *Professional Development Today*, Vol 4 (2), pp. 43–54.

Carnell, E. and Lodge, C. (2002) *Supporting Effective Learning.* London: Paul Chapman.

Egan, G. (1982) *The Skilled Helper.* Monterey, California: Brooks/Cole.

Fullan, M. (2001) *The New Meaning of Educational Change*, (3rd edition). London: Routledge Falmer.

Harber, C. (2004) *The Violence of Schooling.* London: Paul Chapman.

Hargreaves, A. and Fink, D. (2000) 'The three dimensions of reform', *Educational Leadership*, 57(7), pp.30–34.

Lodge, C. (2003) 'Learning about learning', *CPD Update*, Issue 61, London: Optimus.

Middlewood, D. (2002) *Assessment of Teachers for the 21st Century.* Paper presented to the Third International Education Conference, Athens, May.

Rossman, G., Corbett, H. and Firestone, W. (1998) *Change and Effectiveness in Schools: A Cultural Perspective.* Albany NY: Sunny Press.

Stoll, L., Fink, D. and Earl, L. (2003) *It's About Learning: (and it's About Time)*. London: RoutledgeFalmer.

Senge, P. (1990) *The Fifth Discipline: The Art and Practice of the Learning Organisation*. London: Century Business.

Smith, A., Lovatt, M. and Wise, D. (2003) *Accelerated Learning: A User's Guide*. Stafford: Network Educational Press.

West-Burnham, J. and O'Sullivan, F. (1998) *Leadership and Professional Development in Schools*. London: Financial Times/Pitman.

Chapter 2

Why Learning Schools Are Needed

Preview

This chapter considers the following questions:

- What is the importance of an emphasis on learning in this century?
- What is the influence of a global perspective on education?
- What are the inadequacies of past and current practice and the implications of a failure to change?

> *The analogy that might make the student's view more comprehensible to adults is to imagine oneself on a ship sailing across an unknown sea, to an unknown destination. An adult would be desperate to know where he/she is going. But a child only knows he is going to school ... The chart is neither available nor understandable to him/her ... Very quickly, the daily life on board ship becomes all important ... The daily chores, the demands, the inspections, become the reality, not the voyage, nor the destination.*
>
> Mary Alice White (1971)

Why a new emphasis on learning is needed

Ask members of the public what schools are for and the vast majority will reply using one of three phases:

(a) To teach children.
(b) So that children can learn.
(c) To educate children.

The word 'educate' is a broad one and implies that those using it leave the means to the schools themselves but the balance or choice between 'teaching' and 'learning' in schools has become a matter of considerable debate, especially in the last decade of the last century and the early years of this one. Perhaps inevitably, as a new century, and indeed millennium, approached, many writers and educationalists looked forward to the needs of a new era in the twenty-first century. Many of these arguments centre upon the changing needs of the world and individual societies in this century, the vastly different circumstances which face people in the future and, particularly, the unpredictability of that future. What many schools have successfully provided was seen as no longer appropriate or adequate for this future and this is linked with a fundamental shift in thinking about the relative significance of teaching and learning.

In 1980, Carl Rogers set out the characteristics of what we shall call 'a teaching school'. The main principles were:

- teachers have the knowledge: pupils receive the knowledge imparted to them;
- tests and examinations measure the extent to which pupils have received;
- teachers have the authority in the classroom; pupils obey – they do not work effectively unless the teacher controls and directs them;
- teachers determine the goals for pupils;
- the intellect is central to success.

(Based on Rogers, 1980)

It is easy to see what the characteristics of a school based on these principles would include:

- learning is a product – what you have learned;
- conformity would be encouraged – dissent is unacceptable;
- labelling (e.g. of those who do not 'fit') becomes self-fulfilling;
- structures are rigid – what you learn is prescribed;
- compartmentalisation exists in age groupings;
- performance is seen as all important;
- emphasis is on rational thinking and on knowledge from established sources.

Later, it may be helpful to you to return to this list and think about how many of these characteristics exist in your school at present.

New developments

There are a number of developments in the past 15–20 years which have had an influence on our thinking about the relative emphasis in learning and teaching. These include the following (all of which are dealt with in following chapters in this book):

- increasing discovery of how the brain works (it is claimed that 80 per cent of all we know about the human brain has been found out since 1990!);
- ideas of multiple intelligence, rather than a fixed entity of intelligence;
- understanding of the different learning styles that individuals have;
- recognition of the importance of emotions or emotional intelligence (Golman, 1996);

- realisation of the large number of factors that affect individuals' capacity to learn (diet, physical environment, time of day etc);
- influence of ICT.

All these, and others, have shown us the extreme limitations of the assumption behind the teaching school described above. If you add to these the political and sociological developments related to education, particularly the notion of inclusiveness, there are overwhelming arguments for trying to ensure that our educational systems and their institutions reshape themselves so that their focus is firmly on learning, first and foremost. Hence, the need for schools to be 'learning schools'.

Relationship between learning and teaching

Whereas in the teaching school the basic assumption was that you needed to be taught to learn something, we need to understand that:

- teaching can take place without learning occurring;
- and learning can take place without any teaching.

First, teaching can have any of the following learning outcomes:

(a) It may efficiently transfer knowledge to learners who put this to use in tests or examinations.
(b) It may inspire learners to go away and develop what they have learned and apply it in other areas.
(c) It may induce no learning at all (except the conviction that school is 'boring', 'irrelevant', 'a waste of time').
(d) Or it may encourage those being taught to learn that there are certain 'rules' that enable you to survive or even do quite well at school.

These include:

- keep quiet and you won't get into trouble;
- look as if you are concentrating hard and you won't get asked too many questions;
- do any copying from books thoroughly;
- in general, do what most other people are doing;
- make your work very neat and well laid out even if you think it may not be correct;
- do the minimum required, enough to avoid trouble.

These may appear cynical but research has shown that thousands of children in our schools learn the processes which enable them to be relatively unnoticed. Have you ever tried shadowing a pupil through a day or more in a secondary school? Those who have (including the authors of this book) have found children or young people who went through a whole day or more (up to three days in one case) without uttering a single word in class. In most cases, these learners had adopted (probably unconsciously) the above 'rules'. One imagines when they arrived home and a parent asked 'what did you do at school today' that the answer familiar to many parents 'nothing much' was more truthful than might be thought.

However, learning also takes place without teaching. Most of our learning outside of school, as well as post-school, college or university learning, does not give us an official teacher (except in such situations as organised adult education classes of course). Yet we all know that we go on learning throughout our lives. How do we do this?

- we learn by watching others, sometimes formally sitting or working alongside someone else who is doing something, or informally just by noting what someone else does;
- we learn by advice or tips from others;
- we learn by reading, watching television, exploring the internet;
- we learn by trial and error;
- most of all, we learn by doing. From our daily experiences we, often unconsciously, review, draw conclusions, conceptualise, adjust our practice.

This kind of learning all takes place in contexts which:

- are *real*;
- and *relevant*.

This means the context is not artificial or hypothetical; the consequences of our learning or our failure to learn have a direct impact on our lives.

We also learn to manage our lives, most people perfectly successfully, while remaining ignorant in a huge number of areas. We do this through developing learning strategies.

Think of some areas of life in which you are incompetent! Don't worry, all of us as mature adults are useless in certain things. The authors of this book, all well qualified and we believe intelligent, listed these as some of the things that we are no good at (although we are not saying whose is which!):

- *cooking;*
- *dealing with a car breakdown;*
- *dancing;*
- *household money management;*
- *do-it-yourself work;*
- *understanding opera;*
- *finding your way round a strange area.*

We have done this exercise with many teachers and support staff and the list is usually considerable. The next step is to ask 'how have you managed to be successful mature adults whilst being useless at so many things?' In other words, what learning strategies have you developed? You might like to jot down yours. The commonest ones given are:

- get someone else to do it for you (far and away the commonest);
- avoid situations where your ignorance will be shown (the second commonest);
- bluff (the third commonest and as one person pointed it, this makes you a knowledgeable expert in waffle!);
- pretend or convince yourself that such things are not important (the fourth commonest and it can include belittling the skills which you do not have).

Knowing what your weaknesses are, as well as your strengths, is a crucial part of our learning and successful experience. We can then make decisions about what to do about them and develop strategies to manage effectively in those areas where we are not so strong. Dubin (1962) developed a model, which is adapted here.

The unconscious incompetent: the person who is no good at something but does not know this. This person is never going to learn! This is why when we counsel or mentor someone, we start by saying 'how do you think it went?', hoping that the person will show their own awareness of their weakness or problem. If they do, they are:
The conscious incompetent: you know you are not good at something, but your being aware of this makes you likely to be in a good state for learning. As you begin to learn, perhaps by trying something new, you are becoming:
The conscious competent: you can do something but you are aware of each step you take. At a later stage, when you are used to the change, you may well become:
The unconscious competent: you can do something automatically, as if on autopilot. This is what we do for much of our work and lives in the areas in which we have become proficient. However, there are dangers because at some point we just assume we are doing something well and may not notice when we are not.

Driving is a good example. Most people start learning to drive knowing they have it all to learn (conscious incompetent). As they progress, they learn the techniques but are conscious of what they are doing, especially up to and including the driving test! (Conscious competent.) Having passed the test and been driving for a few years, most of us are driving on autopilot when we get into our cars (unconscious competent). However, road accident research shows that over 70 per cent of drivers are not as good as they think they are and

---

Case example

Dissatisfied with the quality of work being handed in as homework, some of it obviously done with no understanding, and also conscious of the time wasted to produce inaccurate or poor work, one school in the East Midlands in England changed its strategy to one of positively encouraging students to seek help from others in doing homework or 'out of hours study' as it was called. The main features of the strategy were:

- if the student had an elder sibling he/she should seek help from them and if that sibling had done that work or similar previously, so much the better;
- students should get in touch with other students to find out how they had got on with the task, what they had put for answers/solutions etc;
- the students would record which other students they had sought help from or given help to on the work they handed in;
- follow up and feedback on the homework involved not only the work itself but what had been learned through the collaboration;
- credit was given for both the work produced, the way help had been sought, help that had been given, and what had been learned.

It is important to note that the school's policy was that those students who completed the task without help could gain as much credit as those who had sought help. The principle to be encouraged was to learn when help was needed – that is in itself a key learning strategy.

---

frequently make errors. Many of those tell the police and the courts that they were doing nothing wrong (unconscious incompetent).

If we could become aware of our strengths and weaknesses in learning while still young (i.e. at school) and develop learning strategies, how much more effective it would be for people. For example, the strategy of 'getting someone else to do it for you', which all of us appear to use in adult life, is positively discouraged in many schools, and the wrong lesson is learned.

Schools with learning at the centre

The twenty-first century is already offering – and will continue to offer – new challenges to us as individuals, members of families, employees and employers, members of communities, societies and nations. We do not even know what some of the challenges will be. As Dalin and Rust expressed it in their book *Towards Schooling in the Twenty First Century*, published in 1996, they envisaged that the task of the school of the future

*assumes that teachers, students and others, often must work with assignments
where there is no known answer or with an approach where the solution is not fully
known.*

(p.153)

However, Dalin and Rust did offer a list of possible challenges for the student:

- to develop and live in a multicultural society;
- to develop a practical and living partnership between genders;
- to develop and take responsibility for local surroundings;
- to take responsibility for the physical environment and understand the consequences of an ecological perspective in daily life;
- to understand possibilities and dangers related to an advanced economic/ technological society;
- to work for peace and prevent war;
- to live and take responsibility for a multigenerational society;
- to understand media language, and how to cope with the flood of information confronting humankind;
- to understand differences in conditions of life, and work for a fair and just world;
- to understand the internationalising tendencies and learn to take responsibility to live and function in an international society;
- to understand the dynamics in work and industry, to learn to create an active relationship to work life and the challenges that wait when a major focus of life is work;
- and to take advantage of a boundless learning market, and become capable of developing an individual learning plan, which incorporates co-operation between student, home and teacher and takes advantage of the electronic market.

(Dalin and Rust, 1996 p.152)

Thus, we need to ask ourselves first:

*what kinds of people will be best placed to thrive or survive, help others to thrive or
survive, in such a world?*

We suggest that the qualities such people will need include (not in any particular order):

- resilience;
- emotional self-awareness;
- adaptability and flexibility;
- being at ease with uncertainty;
- empathy with others;
- optimistic outlook.

Others can be added of course.

This is an ideal list and no one person will possess them all, hence the importance of different genders, of team and group support, of different cultural dimensions and so on. Nevertheless, such a list can provide a starting point for those trying to set out what education should be striving for.
The second question is:

how can schools play an effective part in helping people during the compulsory schooling period of their lives in preparing them to become such people?

Perhaps the answer to the second question includes, by helping them:

- to *be* effective learners while at school;
- to understand that learning will remain central to their future lives' success;
- to know sufficient about themselves as a learner to want to go on and to be able to go on applying and developing this self-knowledge throughout life.

The significance and importance of school learning therefore is that it harmonises in various ways with the learning that utilises everyday activities and insights. In this way, students' learning is most effective when they can relate what they learn to something else in their experience. Learning schools of the twenty-first century need to be less artificial as organisations, less cut off from what goes on outside them, and the learning that takes place within them needs to be felt and perceived as relevant by all those concerned. When we say 'less cut off', this in the future means not just from our immediate locality and community, but from the international world we live in.

Globalisation

Globalisation cannot be ignored in thinking about how learning schools of the future can be at their most effective. However, the term can be used to refer to:

- *a cultural dimension* – whereby western cultures (especially American) influence local cultures throughout the world;
- *a political dimension* – whereby dimensions have international implications, often overriding national or regional ones;
- *an economic dimension* – whereby market-driven approaches are spread everywhere and prosperity and deprivation are clearly linked across the globe;
- *a technological dimension* – whereby electronic technologies link the corners of the world and underpin all of the above, especially the economic;
- *an environmental dimension* – whereby, as we all live on the same planet, the effects of action in one part will have consequences for all other parts.

The understanding of the interconnectedness of all of us on our planet is crucial to the future of us all and must therefore play a part in the learning and understanding of twenty-first century citizens. Harter's (2000) global village composition powerfully brings home this point to those for example in a European country who wish to focus exclusively on 'home grown' needs. Harter points out that as this century began, if the earth's population could be seen as a village of 100 people, with the ratios exactly the same, the village population would comprise:

- 57 Asians; 21 Europeans; 14 from the western hemisphere, both north and south; 8 Africans;
- 52 would be female; 48 would be male;
- 70 would be non-white; 30 would be white;
- 70 would be non-Christian; 30 would be Christian;
- 89 would be heterosexual; 11 would be homosexual;
- 6 people would possess 59 per cent of the entire world's wealth and all 6 would be from the US;
- 80 would live in substandard housing;
- 70 would be unable to read;
- 50 would suffer from malnutrition.

(Harter, 2000)

Paradoxically, this interconnectedness has also led to greater struggles and conflicts at local levels. Stoll et al (2003, p. 9) describe this well:

> In a world of complexity, instability and unpredictability, people are struggling to make sense of the changes, and to situate themselves within the new milieu. Just as globalisation can destabilise nation states and democratic institutions in the pursuit of profit, tribalism can undermine them in the name of meaning and identity.
>
> This 'greater hunger' has motivated large elements of previously marginalised populations, such as women, racial and ethnic groups, the poor and disabled, to seek more meaningful places in our nations and in the world. It has also contributed to an increase in membership in fundamentalist versions of all the major religions that offer security, predictability and stability in a rapidly changing and somewhat scary world.

Cogan and Derricott (2000) summarised the views from nine different countries on necessary characteristics of twenty-first century citizens as being:

- looking at problems in a global context;
- working co-operatively and responsibly;
- accepting cultural differences;
- thinking in a critical and systematic way;
- solving conflicts non-violently;

- changing lifestyle to protect the environment;
- defending human rights;
- participating in politics.

We may ask ourselves the question: How many of these are fostered through the current educational system and the assessment procedures it requires?

Most of the chapters of this book deal with some of the ways in which these ideas and others mentioned earlier may be achieved, whilst acknowledging that we need to start from wherever we are and all schools are not at the same starting point. We need to be aware of what may be some of the consequences of failing to change to put learning at the centre of our schools.

Implications of a failure to change

(i) The context

Because of the context within which schools (and other educational organisations such as colleges or universities) have been forced to operate, there has been an overwhelming pressure on *achievement*. This is of course a good thing in itself but it is the way in which achievement has been measured and defined, thereby also defining success and failure, that has led to an obsession with standards. Schools have been forced to play 'the standards game' (Gleeson and Gunter, 2001 p.45) to obtain narrow outcomes which can be assessed in tests and examination results. One headteacher writes, in 2001, of 11 years as a head in England:

> *The focus on systems, standards, inputs and outputs, data and accountability has been relentless ... I struggle to recall a piece of legislation which, when implemented, would have increased children's enjoyment of education and made them want to come to school more.*
>
> (Arrowsmith, 2001 p.21)

Why has this happened?

> *Somewhere along the way, in the name of educational reform, policy makers may have confused structure with purpose, measurement with accomplishment, means with ends, compliance with commitment, and teaching with learning.*
>
> (Stoll et al, 2003 p.185)

All this has led to a concentration on how students and their teachers and schools 'perform', and this huge emphasis on performance in these limited terms and the 'performativity culture' which develops in the concern to deliver it is often anti-reflection because of the urgency that there is to reach the required performance levels. Here is one quote from a teacher indicating some of these consequences:

I don't have the job satisfaction now I once had working with young kids because I feel every time I do something intuitive I just feel guilty about it. 'Is this right; am I doing this the right way; does this cover what I am supposed to be covering; should I be doing something else; should I be more structured; should I have this in place; should I have done this?' You start to query everything you are doing – there's a kind of guilt in teaching at the moment. I don't know if that's particularly related to Ofsted but of course it's multiplied by the fact that Ofsted is coming in because you get in a panic that you won't be able to justify yourself when they finally arrive.

(Quoted in Jeffrey and Woods, 1998 p.118)

And here is a quotation from an interview with a student:

A student was explaining why she liked her maths lessons. She was able to perform the problem-solving tasks her teacher set to the required level of attainment in 20 minutes, leaving her 15 minutes to talk with her friends before the end of the lesson.

(Quoted in Elliott, 2001 p.198)

She was prepared to play the standards game so that she could then get on with real matters!

Currently the demand for public accountability places pressures and demands on students which get in the way of effective learning. The public examination system in the UK, for example, is outmoded, unwieldy, prone to inaccuracy and very expensive. Over £250 million pounds was spent in the UK on administering a system which is geared to credentialing rather than encouraging learning and which fewer and fewer people – most notably students – have any real faith in. There are other – more telling – costs. A survey in 2004 revealed that one in eight UK children *under* 12 years is taking some form of drugs to treat depression, and during the 2003 'exam season', over 9,000 calls were received by charities and support services from young people feeling suicidal or very depressed.

(ii) What might this mean?

What 'messages' or 'lessons' may a large number of students in schools under present conditions be taking into the future?

• That formal schooling is a ritual you are required to go through (like the maths student above) before you get on to real life. Some students accept this, enjoy the rituals and play the game successfully in terms of what the outcomes are. Others may see the ritual as irrelevant and meaningless, and may drop out altogether. Others see it as something to be endured before they can escape to 'real life' when schooling ends.

- That there is basically one way (the 'correct' way) to do things, including one way to learn. This one way is heavily dependent upon the teacher.
- That, if you want to improve, the way is to absorb more knowledge and that the improvement will be recognised by an improved grade or number.
- That love of product (Willmott, 1992) is the most important thing; how you gained or achieved the product is much less important.
- That learning is essentially utilitarian.
- That, if all else fails, figures can be manipulated and there is a thin line between 'being creative' and 'cheating' in this context.

This may seem exaggerated but it would be a brave teacher or headteacher who, in the present climate, could claim *never* to have put the best possible gloss on statistics which were for public consumption.

Of course, many students in our schools do not fit this picture but, unless the emphasis in our schools is shifted away from 'the technicist, managerialist and mechanistic' (Gleeson and Gunter, 2001 p.151), generations of adults may emerge who will never meet any of the criteria for prospering in or even coping with the world of this century. Already, these who work in education know how difficult it can be trying to engage parents in their children's education because the parents' own experience of schooling was painful and one of failure.

(iii) One example

In education systems where prescription comes from governments, what inevitably emerges is the notion of the 'one-fit-for-all' approach. Examples in the UK include:

- national strategies (including a 'literacy hour');
- performance management;
- Ofsted's model of teaching;
  and many more.

It is not that any of these is not helpful and/or can be very effective. What they convey, however, is the message that there is *one* way of doing things – which the experience of effective teachers and effective schools have shown is manifestly *not* the case. This approach may be essential because the purpose is to achieve certain predetermined, measurable outcomes (as already mentioned). But the education and development of humans is simply not like that! As Preedy (2001 p.94) has pointed out:

> *Many of the most valuable outcomes of education are multidimensional, complex and long term and cannot be represented by test scores.*

Most teachers – and indeed parents – will also be able to describe some 'unplanned' and 'unexpected' outcomes!

The message that those going through the school system may take into the rest of their lives – that there is one set way of doing things, tackling problems, dealing with situations, gaining new knowledge – is the worst possible one for life in this fast-changing world. Of course many people will discover the real truth for themselves and become adept at these things. How much better though if schooling could be experienced as something where you learn this truth in childhood, adolescence and young adulthood!

Watkins (2004) has summarised the research of many people over many years into what are the inherent attitudes and beliefs about our approaches to learning and education when we operate within a 'performance orientation':

- we believe that ability leads to success;
- we are concerned to be seen as able, and to perform well in others' eyes;
- we seek satisfaction from doing better than others;
- we emphasise competition, public evaluation;
- when the task is difficult we display helplessness: 'I can't do X'.

All this shows a concern for **proving** one's competence and therefore he concludes that this performance orientation can actually depress performance! (Watkins, 2004.)

The purposes of learning and education

At the beginning of this chapter, we suggested three answers that member of the public were likely to give if asked what schools are for. However, beyond that lies the fundamental question of what are the purposes of learning that is gained at school. One of the authors has suggested elsewhere that schools should ideally facilitate:

- learning as a means to an end;
- learning as a process, learning how to learn;
- and learning which provides knowledge which is worth pursuing for its own sake.

(Middlewood, 2005)

There is no doubt that that purpose of learning and education has come to be perceived in most countries as a means to an end, essentially as something utilitarian. Up to and including the 1970s, for example, thousands of young people in developed countries such as the UK, USA, Australia, Canada and others went from school to university to study a subject because they liked, even loved, that subject and wished to spend three years or more reading and examining it in depth. Surveys in the 1990s and this decade show that students above all are motivated by the extent to which a higher qualification will give them a better job, career and financial prospects. (See for example Ivy, 2004). In developing countries, it would be impossible to ignore the fact that educational attainment is the passport to economic success and a higher place in social status, and it would be hypocritical to criticise such desires in those contexts. However, this is not only true in poorer countries. Sugimine (1998 p.121) describes the desperate competition in Japan to get children into the 'right' streams, turning schools into 'fast-grinding and knowledge-based institutions even at elementary level'.

The universities and people seeking the highest qualifications are only one example. What is known as vocational education provides another. The world in which we live will become increasingly driven by technology but it seems certain that people who perform certain tasks will remain essential to our well-being. Examples include:

- people who cut and style our hair;
- people who maintain and mend our boilers, taps, etc;
- people who maintain our parks and gardens;
- people who build our walls, conservatories, etc;
- people who repair our machines – cars to lawnmowers.

Hairdressers, plumbers, gardeners, bricklayers and mechanics are just some of many hundreds of occupations which require particular skills. These skills have to be acquired and regularly updated. Young people need to have the opportunity to acquire these to an appropriate level during the years of schooling.

However, the same principle applies here as in more so-called academic education. At the time of writing, an acute shortage of plumbers has been identified in the UK and several institutions are recruiting people onto relevant courses to meet the demand. But those who become plumbers solely as a means to the end of earning large sums of money are less likely to find satisfaction in the actual work they do, than those who wish to do the work as also some kind of service and who enjoy the processes involved. Bricklayers also are in short supply. Stories are told of those bricklayers who see themselves as:

- laying row on row of bricks to make walls;
- or helping to create buildings;
- or having a vision of what the building looks like at the end.

Learning in any context which is *merely* a means to an end is ultimately unsatisfactory and has all kinds of consequences for the education that is based upon it.

In conclusion

In looking back to the 'teaching school' characterised earlier in the chapter, and looking forward to the 'learning school' of the future, perhaps we may summarise as below.

	Twentieth century teaching school	Twenty-first century learning school
1	Learning is a product.	Learning is a process.
2	Learning at school is complete in itself.	Schooling is a contribution to a life-long learning process.
3	Intelligent, rational and right answers are paramount.	Emotions, instinct, creativity are as important as intellect.
4	Assessment is of outcomes.	Assessment is for learning.
5	Learning takes place at school.	Learning takes place everywhere.
6	Groupings are based on age and ability.	Basis for groupings varies according to learning need.
7	Conformity is crucial to school achievement.	Independence is encouraged.
8	Schools are self-standing institutions.	The school's boundaries are endlessly flexible.
9	Schools and teachers determine goals.	Students determine own goals.
10	Teachers provide and deliver. Pupils and students receive.	Teachers manage and facilitate learning. Pupils and students learn how to learn and apply this to themselves.
11	Teachers are experts.	Teachers are specialists – in teaching – and are learners.
12	Teachers have authority.	Teachers have authoritative presence, based on learning.
13	Professionals provide; parents support.	Parents and others contribute to learning.

References

Arrowsmith, R. (2001) 'A right performance' in D. Gleeson and C. Husbands (eds) *The Performing School*. London: RoutledgeFalmer.

Cogan, J. and Derricott, R. (2000) *Citizenship for the 21st Century: An International Perspective on Education*. London: Kogan Page.

Dalin, P. and Rust, V. (1996) *Towards Schooling in the Twenty First Century*. London: Cassell.

Dubin, R. (1962) *Self Concepts and Training Potential*. London: Pan Books.

Elliot, J. (2001) 'Characteristics of performative cultures' in D. Gleeson and C. Husbands (eds) *The Performing School*. London: RoutledgeFalmer.

Gleeson, D. and Gunter, H. (2001) 'The performing school and the modernisation of teachers' in D. Gleeson and C. Husbands (eds) *The Performing School*. London: RoutledgeFalmer.

Golman, D. (1996) *Emotional Intelligence*. London: Bloomsbury.

Harter, P. (2000) 'Earth's population' in B. Bieler *International News: Inclusion and Universal Co-operation*. www.disabilityworld.org, April–May 2000.

Ivy, J. (2004) 'Teachers who take on more', in *Headship Matters*, no. 27 pp. 11–13.

Jeffrey, B. and Woods, P. (1998) *Testing Teachers: The Effect of School Inspections on Primary Teachers*. London: Falmer Press

Middlewood, D. (2005) 'Leading and managing staff and organisational learning' in T. Bush and D. Middlewood *Leading and Managing People in Education*. London: Paul Chapman.

Preedy, M. (2001) 'Curriculum evaluation: measuring what we value' in D. Middlewood and N. Burton (eds) *Managing the Curriculum*. London: Paul Chapman.

Rogers, C. (1980) *A Way of Being*. Boston: Houghton Mifflin.

Sugimine, H. (1998) 'Primary schooling in Japan' in J. Moyles and L. Hargreaves (eds) *The Primary Curriculum: Learning from International Perspectives*. London: Routledge.

Watkins, C. (2004) 'Learners' orientation to learning', in *Newsbrief*. London: NAPE.

White, M. A. (1971) 'The view from the pupil's desk' in M. Silberman (ed) *The Experience of Schooling*, pp. 337–345. NY: Rinehart and Winston.

Willmott, T. (1992) 'Postmodernism and excellence: the de-differentiation of economy and culture' in *Journal of Organisational Change and Management*, Vol 5 (1), pp. 58–68.

Chapter 3

Leadership for Learning Schools

Preview

This chapter addresses the following questions:

- What are the challenges and potential threats to leadership in new learning schools?
- What demands will be placed on leaders of twenty-first century schools?
- How should we be preparing, recruiting, training and developing the right leaders?
- In a new era, is there a necessity for leadership at all levels?

> *Leadership and learning are indispensable to each other.*
>
> John F. Kennedy

Leadership for learning: the challenge

What makes for effective leadership has always attracted high levels of interest. However, the level of debate, curiosity and experimentation that has been in evidence over the last decade has been unparalleled, reaching its clearest physical statement in the UK in the official launching of the National College for School Leadership in November 2002. There are many reasons for this level of interest but at the heart of the development are three key factors:

1. The nature and demands on school leaders are so very different from anything faced in the past.
2. The well publicised recruitment crisis and its massive implications for schools is being most keenly felt at senior leadership level and headship in particular.
3. The complex question of how best to utilise the rapidly expanding opportunities for developing and harnessing genuinely effective teaching and learning (not least the rapid advances in the educational technologies) has raised dramatically the profile, role and influence of school leaders.

School leaders can no longer restrict their ambition to providing a good education for their own students within the confines of the traditional school day. They need to create structures and pathways to allow open access for the local and wider community as well as promoting and encouraging teachers to enhance their own learning. The ever quickening pace of technological development has already presented a huge range of opportunities to think imaginatively and strategically about how to put schools at the heart of learning communities. Leaders of new learning schools will, however, have to throw off any inhibitions about what is possible if they are to embrace fully the enormous implications of what is already available in terms of teaching and learning and what may be accessible in the future.

Current barriers to leadership for learning

The increased pressures brought on by successive governments determined to prove to voters that they both value education and have policies to improve its quality have placed enormous demands on teachers. As a consequence they are increasingly opting for a life outside school and turning down promotion. Fewer and fewer younger teachers with real leadership potential seem prepared to consider taking on leadership roles in schools at a time when the majority of the cohort currently occupying senior leadership roles are within ten years of retirement.

Added to this, a major irony of the last two decades is that much of the more recent agenda targeted at school improvement has restricted a head's ability to develop the skill set necessary to meet the requirements of new learning schools. There have been many confusing messages emanating from government:

- *take control but follow central directives;*
- *be imaginative but make sure that your teachers follow this or that clearly defined strategy;*
- *innovate, take risks, experiment – but on no account fail;*
- *above all, be transformational leaders whilst we, the government, bombard you with transactional duties!*

Informed prescription – informed professionalism

The head of the UK government's Delivery Unit has spoken in various public forums about the government's move in the last two to three years from informed prescription to informed professionalism, i.e. giving school leaders the trust, power and means to transform the learning agenda. The truth is that a great deal of the evidence – audits, Ofsted inspections, league tables, national strategies etc – point to an overriding culture that is still heavily centralist and directive in tone, a culture in fact that still does not trust school leaders to take *real* responsibility for moving the agenda for change forward.

Currently, much of a headteacher's role is concerned with management rather than leadership activities. Most headteachers spend relatively little time in classrooms with students and even less analysing the quality of teaching and learning in evidence. Their duties include:

- personnel;
- buildings maintenance;
- crisis management;
- staffing and recruitment;
- budgetary management;
- bidding for funding;
- examination analysis;
- dealing with the sometimes bewildering array of external agencies which have a vested interest in schools etc.

Where, however, is *learning* in this list? Where is the opportunity for headteachers to develop their own learning as well as the learning of others?

Not enough time!

The reality is that there appears to be precious little time available to do what must be the school leader's core business of auditing, analysing and enhancing the quality of learning. In order to become genuine lead learners, school leaders will need time to reflect on current and potential practice. Proactive secondments, for example, focused on action research, have long been identified as essential and worthwhile opportunities for school leaders to reassess and re-examine their beliefs and prejudices. Such opportunities should no longer be the stuff of political ideological dreams. If headteachers are going to *promote* learning properly they must also *engage in* their own learning. Such learning must be real, uncluttered and closely structured to ensure that they will develop the confidence to question their built in assumptions about what does or does not work in learning schools.

Case example one

Action research – time out

Shortly after it began operating, the National College for School Leadership launched its Research Associateship programme. This programme allows senior leaders to pursue an area of personal interest and disseminate the outcomes that impact on practice; it gives them an opportunity to study, have time for reflection and make a valid contribution to the development of the College. It is widely regarded as one of the most valuable and worthwhile of the College's initiatives and the research publications have attracted a significant amount of interest.

A new era

Bowring-Carr and West-Burnham (1997 p.120) believe that schools now exist:

in a state of permanent tension between the apparent simplicity of surface structures and the deep complexity of leading and learning.

They identify four trends which have been instrumental in bringing about this new era of change:

- schools are increasingly vulnerable, working as they do in the glare of public accountability;
- the increased emphasis on, for example, value added, value for money, year on year improvement, downgrades the view of learning as an iterative process;
- important changes in the way society operates inevitably affect fundamentally the manner and nature of how schools respond to and operate within those changes;
- there is a growing awareness that in a significantly more complex and chaotic world, schools reflect that huge and demanding range of variables more keenly than other much less people-centred organisations.

If strategic leadership in schools is going to meet these challenges and produce systems and structures which will both recognise and respond imaginatively to the learning needs which are demanded by the age in which we now live, it must create learning (including e-learning) communities for students and teachers which will satisfy a knowledge-based society and economy and encourage all those engaged in the process to celebrate and endorse an active view of learning.

Headlearners: broadening horizons

The increasingly complex and competitive demands facing school leaders in the twenty-first century highlight a real need to concentrate less on the *mechanics of teaching* and more on *student learning*. A rapidly growing body of research is emerging which is suggesting strongly that schools need to adopt learning-centred leadership if standards are going to continue to rise and create gateways for the widest possible access to lifelong learning. It is in no way fanciful or far-fetched to say that in order to achieve the objective of enabling young people to become effective, efficient and flexible learners, headteachers will need to concentrate less on being headteachers and far more on becoming headlearners.

However, even in these supposedly modern times, the reaction of some to such a concept is to be both disbelieving and scornful. Francis Bennion reports the following exchange, under the heading 'Education Gimmickry':

I recently received a letter from the Sarah Bonnell School, an inner London secondary school at Stratford. It came from a person described in the letterhead as 'Ms Cauthar Maryam Latif Tooley, Headlearner/Headteacher'. Earlier I had queried Ms Tooley's use of the term Headlearner on the ground that it was a foolish gimmick. In the letter Ms Tooley denied this. She took very seriously her position as one who was learning along with the students.

Francis Bennion. Website 'In Parliament' (2004)

Relegating the concept of headlearner to the level of gimmickry would seem to suggest that even though we are already in the current millennium the rationale behind the thinking of headlearner is still capable of eliciting some anger and ridicule.

The power of charisma!

Surely, it is argued, if standards are going to be maintained and the necessary improvements outlined in UK government directives are going to be secured, schools need to be run by powerful, omniscient, charismatic figureheads who dominate and dictate the culture of their respective organisations! However, such a view is challenged by equally powerful voices, not least those emanating from the National College for School Leadership (2004 p.3):

It is now widely recognised that the traditional model of school leadership, that of the headteacher as a powerful, heroic, single teacher, is becoming outmoded and is unlikely to deliver future reform agendas set by successive governments.

It is of course possible that the autocratic superhead may have been able to put in place sustained organisational systems which effectively managed the transfer of knowledge from teacher to learner. It is also relatively straightforward for a headteacher to have a real influence on the conditions and the culture of the organisation and on easily identifiable factors such as attendance and behaviour. It is much more difficult to see how such an approach can encourage the dialogue, ownership and shared responsibility for learning which will need to be at the centre of new learning schools.

Emphasising the importance of learning

Leaders of twenty-first century schools will need to have the will and the expertise to recognise, cultivate and encourage effective learning. For that to happen, they will need to take on and run with the essential truth that the best learning experiences start where the *learner* is, not where the *teacher* is – and that point of view challenges much of what has been at the root of educational practice for a very long time!

Bowring-Carr and West-Burnham (1999 p.135) see the headteacher as the steward of learning:

Through personal example, in conversation, in notes to other colleagues, in some of the items in agendas for meetings, in every conceivable way, the leader will demonstrate an unending commitment to learning, personal and professional; the steward of learning will put in place those structures that say overtly that here learning is vital and honoured.

Stoll et al (2003), in setting out seven holistic modes for 'leaders for learning' would endorse their view that there is a built-in demand for such leaders to enhance their own learning as well as that of others. They must, therefore:

- lead by example in encouraging formal and informal questioning of the status quo, providing students and staff with every incentive and opportunity to develop their own learning and challenge others to do the same;
- stress to everyone involved in the educational debate that nothing should be taken for granted or accepted as fact;
- give learners in an organisation the confidence and the wherewithal to research and broaden their knowledge base;
- put research and enquiry at the centre of everything they do.

Given these trends, it is not surprising that the demands and expectations placed on leadership in schools have grown and changed. Leithwood et al (1999 p.188) stress the extent to which leadership for learning needs to be at the heart of an organisation:

Much of the contribution that leaders make to the learning depends on properties of the school organisation, over which they have considerable control – mission, cultures, structures and resources for example. Collective capacity development on a broad scale depends on building conditions into each of these organisational properties that not only do not inhibit, but also create the opportunities.

Leadership in learning schools will, therefore, only be perceived as being effective if it enables all real and potential stakeholders to be transformed into *focused and efficient* learners, able to find out, take in and give out information in the sure knowledge that they are comfortable with and fully engaged in the learning process.

Different priorities ...

If headteachers are first and foremost concerned with where their school will figure in the next set of published performance tables, they will more likely be cautious, unadventurous and disinclined to make the fundamental step change that is required to create genuine learning opportunities for current and future generations. Dimmock (2003 p.9) makes the point unequivocally:

Learning centred schools prompt a major shift in the mindset of leaders away from business matters to the centrality of students and learning. They become goal oriented in respect of improving student learning outcomes, interpreting their work roles and judging their performance in terms of the contribution they make to enhancing learning.

Moving the mindset away therefore from business matters to student learning is a task that requires organisations to look at new leadership and management structures. Traditional hierarchical management models reflect a culture that is essentially transactional in approach where the emphasis is on the establishment of order and the maintenance of clearly defined structures and routines. New learning schools will require different approaches, different priorities and structures which are flatter, more democratic and very specifically geared to the promotion of learning.

Case example two

Bishop Stopford School: leadership at all levels
Following on from a seminar about developing a professional learning community, headteacher Margaret Holman and her leadership team abandoned their traditional management model for one which allowed time and space to target school improvement and create what they described as a professional learning community. The established management model did not encourage coherent thinking or promote shared responsibility for learning. (See Figures 3.1 and 3.2)

Figure 3.1 *The management model (Holman, 2004).*

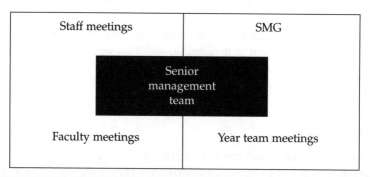

The new model, with its core activites at the centre, puts learning at the heart of the organisation and encourages a corporate responsibility for improvement.

Figure 3.2 *The leadership model (Holman, 2004).*

Staff development		Self evaluation	
MBA group	Seminar groups	Staff forum
Internal secondments	School development group	Associate staff forum
Teaching and learning teams	Year team meetings	Faculty meetings

School improvement

Leadership

Learning community

Leadership for learning: building the capacity

Headteachers have to create a genuine sense of shared leadership across the whole organisation. They must not only encourage a climate of ongoing formal learning on the part of all staff, they need also to lead by example. The case for headteacher sabbaticals has already been made – time out to reflect, research and broaden one's knowledge base about what opportunities and strategies for cultivating and encouraging learning already exist and what may be possible in the future. It is also important that they:

- take advantage of the increasing number of leadership programmes and qualifications now available;
- challenge embedded prejudices;
- improve learning opportunities for others by consistently encouraging and championing the importance of school-based action research;
- manage the required move from 'improving schools' to 'learning organisations' sensitively and with great clarity.

If a school is therefore determined to take up the challenge of broadening horizons and developing people's skills to carry on learning in the future, it will have to adopt leadership structures and strategies which promote learning at all levels. It will in fact have to be much more resourceful and imaginative in drawing all members of the organisation into leadership roles, not only equipping them to carry out tasks of the moment but also giving them the confidence to take on initiatives in the future. Effective leaders produce effective leaders at all levels. A really good headteacher will leave an organisation with the necessary skills, confidence and knowledge to carry on his/her work. An ineffective leader may through direct action and force of personality be able to run a successful ship for a time. But if holes appear and he is unable to fill them, in all likelihood the ship will sink.

Intuitive leadership: transformational change

The challenges facing schools will require leaders who are far more than solid, safe professionals, comfortable with the status quo and who lean instinctively towards transactional leadership. Instead, they will require gifted and passionate strategic thinkers who are comfortable with and naturally good at transformational change. This is the nature and quality of leadership required for new learning schools and yet the evidence to date is that the market for such leadership is a rapidly diminishing one. Assuming that the situation may not be as serious as this, an additional major factor is the matter of recruitment and selection of the next generation of school leaders. The traditional methods for recognising, nurturing and then choosing those people who have a natural affinity for and ability in leading others have largely been unimaginative and formula driven. All too often selecting teachers up to and including headteachers has relied far too much on chance, convenience and, most worryingly of all, ill-informed opinion.

Governing bodies do not have a convincing track record of calculated risk-taking where recruitment at senior leadership level is concerned. As a consequence there has been and still is too much reliance on the assessment of candidates' knowledge and skills, qualities required for primarily transactional management. Leaders of new learning schools will need to be judged much more on their ability to inspire and enthuse people, qualities which come much more from their values and attributes. An increasing body of research literature is beginning to consider in depth the extent to which leadership is intuitive, how much in fact comes from a person's life history, i.e. who they are, what they have been. The emphasis here is much less on the characteristics of leadership and much more on the characters of leaders – less on the 'how and what' and more on the 'who and why' of leadership.

In order to bring about the revolutionary implications of the move away from didactic teaching to proactive learning, those leading and managing the move must be passionately involved and intuitively geared towards creating naturally an environment in which people will feel excited, empowered and confident enough to give up long held views and approaches about what makes for an effective school. They must encourage:

- innovation;
- experimentation;

- risk-taking;
- occasional failure;
- perseverance.

Transactional leaders comfortable with day to day management tasks, secure in the known and understood, wary and sceptical of change, will not in their wildest dreams be able to do it.

Making the change

Establishing the positive learning environment

It almost goes without saying that new learning schools will not be able to promote positive learning in old, worn-out buildings. There is already plenty of (literally) concrete evidence that schools now being built through the Building Schools for the Future programme are carrying on the pioneering work of the City Technology Colleges initiative insofar as much more thought is being given to ways in which buildings can enhance learning.

- Lead learners will have to play an integral role in ensuring that, for example, ICT developments and the intelligent deployment and use of the potential of e-learning are wholly focused on improving the learning.
- There needs to be imaginative and flexible use of the workforce to ensure that everyone with a contribution to the learning agenda is trained and fully utilised.
- School leaders will have to challenge and change the narrow view which would claim that the only relevant experience for a child is to be taught by a fully qualified teacher. New learning schools will not be precious about who can contribute to student learning. Instead they will practise a philosophy which celebrates the fact that:
  - everyone is capable of learning something new;
  - everyone is capable of teaching another individual;
  - every member of the organisation is a valuable learning resource.

Headteachers have certain unique responsibilities but their most important role is to *celebrate* and *support* a culture where it is both natural and exciting for people to make learning real, relevant and challenging. High expectations alongside rigorous accountability tied to no blame will be motivators for those staff who genuinely see change and challenge as presenting opportunities rather than threats. If a school is going to pursue an agenda for dynamic learning, it must operate within a cultural climate of self-empowerment operating through distributed leadership. Bollingham (1999 p.12) states:

Headteachers will need to create conditions in which the leadership of a wide range of staff is fostered. The role involves striking a balance between providing direction

43

and sharing leadership throughout the school community. Who leads and who follows will depend on expertise and the nature of the process being undertaken rather than on formal position.

It is for this reason that the schools can no longer rely on any system of hierarchical leadership if they are going to re-engineer themselves in order to meet the needs of children living in the present millennium. Hierarchies create dependency but learning is more than anything about encouraging people to take responsibility for their own learning and experiment in the sure knowledge that risking failure in order to discover more about themselves is a strength and not a weakness.

Building the relationships

Fullan (2003 p.24) has stressed that truly effective leaders are those who genuinely promote and sustain a positive ethos of distributed leadership within their respective organisations:

You cannot have highly effective principals unless there is distributed leadership throughout the school. Indeed, fostering leadership at many levels is one of the principal's main roles. School leadership is a team sport.

Only when positive learning relationships are distributed among all staff and a true ethos of collaboration and the sharing of good practice is embedded into the culture will schools be in a position to change and adapt to the needs of the twenty-first century. Only through distributed leadership will schools be able to:

- create and sustain the capacity to maintain developmental work;
- achieve and maintain long-term improvement;
- create positive partnerships with other schools;
- improve learning at all levels;
- cultivate staff who combine a strategic role with a teaching commitment;
- produce future school leaders;
- enhance the quality and relevance of rigorous performance review.

There is no way that school leaders will be able to build these relationships on their own. They must see their organisation with its own character, ethos and levels of expectations as co-existing within a powerful alliance of external partnerships. The National College for School Leadership (2004 p.3) in a recent publication laid down the following pre-conditions for successful partnerships:

- creative thinking;
- aligned incentives;
- a willingness to pursue the tendering process;
- the ability to attract and then negotiate with prospective partners;
- the capacity to undertake partnerships.

Allied to this must be a recognition by all parties that creating genuinely productive partnerships is at once a really difficult but ultimately soluble problem. School leaders will have to be comfortable working in contexts that require entrepreneurial skills and the ability to think in entirely new ways. They will also have to demonstrate the sort of maverick leadership recognised in an increasing number of successful leaders if they are to convince potentially cynical partners that they have a crucial role to play in developing new strategies for learning. This is not something that the commercial world, for example, can afford to miss out on!

Emotional intelligence: leading and managing the implications of change

A recurrent theme of this chapter has been the need for school leaders to have the courage, the confidence, the conviction and the intuition to move the agenda on from teaching centred pedagogy to learning centred practice. There is a demand for fundamental rather than incremental change if such a major shift is going to take place.

- Transactional, competent, safe and essentially centralist leadership, from government down will not do. Leaders of new learning schools will not fit the conventional mould. Fullan (2003 p.75) describes the leaders who will be able to lead and manage the implications of transformational change:

  Compared to high-profile leaders with big personalities who make headlines and become celebrities, the good-to-great leaders seem to have come from Mars. Self-effacing, quiet, reserved, even shy – these leaders are a paradoxical blend of personal humility and professional will. They are more like Lincoln and Socrates than Patton or Caesar.

- Middle leaders too have a vitally important role to play in ensuring that leadership for learning is widely distributed throughout the school. They are the people who perhaps more than any others will move the agenda on from theory to reality. They will need to have a secure grasp of the organisation's key objectives and possess the skill and the wherewithal to play their part in securing those objectives. NCSL launched the 'Leading from the Middle' programme in April 2002 with the express intent of delivering high quality training aimed at building leadership capacity. Fast track initiatives designed to recognise early and promote quickly are intended to equip the right people with the confidence and knowledge to take on leadership roles.

- If schools are genuinely going to take on the responsibility for creating and providing learning organisations they must promote an environment which recognises and nurtures talent, celebrates initiative and motivates individuals to embrace change.

Collins (2001 p.6) makes an important point when he says:

> *The old adage 'People are your most important asset' turns out to be wrong. People are **not** your most important asset. The **right** people are.*

New learning schools will only become a reality if the leaders not only understand the concept of true engagement in learning but also have the ability to educate, lead and inspire others to join the revolution. Closely linked with this must be a full commitment from central government to release schools from the risk-averse culture in which they currently operate, where their measurable performance is constantly under the spotlight, and give them the freedom and confidence to think and plan innovatively about how to turn schools into learning organisations.

And it can be so rewarding! Fullan (2003 p.8) notes:

> *Investing in leaders developing leaders is one of the most exciting and high yield strategic innovations of recent times. We have always known that leaders developing leaders within organisation is essential... The success of a given leadership term is not just impact on the bottom line but on how many good leaders are left behind after the leader's tenure.*

And of course the major advantage of creating a culture where leadership permeates everything is that such a culture promotes equally strongly the practice of shared learning. Such a view is powerfully endorsed by Street (2003 p.1):

> *A shift towards a more distributed approach to school leadership has implications for the way in which schools nurture and develop the skills of their staff. Leaders in schools are exploring more effective ways of increasing their capacity to be proactive in their responses to the challenges facing them in the twenty-first century. The aim is for the school to be able to take control of its own professional learning in order to support its growth.*

Teaching and learning styles: making the investment

- School leaders will only be able to understand the challenges and characteristics of what is meant by new learning schools if they are given every opportunity to invest and develop as a direct result of their own learning. Although such a statement on the one hand appears to be stunningly obvious, the implications are immense.
- There needs to be investment in learning on an unparalleled scale. Strategies need to be put in place which will enable individuals and organisations to have the time and training to participate in targeted action research projects which will broaden horizons and offer relevant and ground breaking approaches to learning.

- All the stakeholders – from central government down – involved in moving the learning agenda forward will need to:
  - feel empowered and valued;
  - be keen to explore the key issues;
  - be sufficiently well informed to put effective improvement plans in place;
  - create an honest and concentrated desire on the part of all the stakeholders to re-establish creativity and enjoyment as prime drivers of a curriculum which in its broadest and most fundamental sense is designed to promote independent learning.

Above all, the mantra must be that a focus on performance can depress performance whereas a focus on learning can enhance performance.

The rapid and increasingly diverse demands facing society over the next 20 years and beyond will mean that teachers and learners will need to reach levels of sophistication and expertise previously unimagined.

The uncertainty and complexity of what lies ahead presents leaders of new learning schools with the task of constructing and delivering a curriculum which will be able to prepare this and future generations with the means whereby they can take on and answer the economic, political, social and moral questions that will be asked of them.

In order to do this, schools will have to become, in a fundamental and wholly new sense, learning organisations. It is a task Bowring-Carr and West-Burnham (1997 p.163) acknowledge as being just about as difficult as they come:

> It is extremely difficult and painful to scrutinise dispassionately bred-in-bones activities and attitudes. To do so requires a total openness and a complete dismantling of all hierarchical structures and forms of thinking; it requires an acceptance that there is no easy reliance on someone 'out there' having a pre-packaged solution.

It is, nonetheless, a task that school leaders will have to take on with conviction and enthusiasm if they are to create twenty-first century schools which will genuinely embrace learning for all.

References

Bollingham, R. (1999) 'Leadership', in M. Brundrett (ed) *Principles of School Management*. Kings Lynn: Peter Francis.

Bowring-Carr, C. and West-Burnham, J. (1997) *Effective Learning in Schools*. London: Pearson Education.

Collins, J. (2001) *Good to Great*: New York: Harper Collins.

Davies, B. and Hentschke, G. (2003) *Public/Private Partnerships in Education*. Nottingham: National College for School Leadership.

Dimmock, C. (2003) 'Leadership in learning centred schools', in M. Brundett, N. Burton and R. Smith (eds) *Leadership in Education*. London: Sage.

Fullan, M. (2003) *The Moral Imperative of School Leadership*. London: Corwin Press.

Holman, M. (2004) 'Leadership at all levels', *Headship Matters*, No. 27, *Leadership*. London: Optimus.

Leithwood, K., Jantzi, D. and Steinbach, T. (1999) *Changing Leadership for Changing Times*. Buckingham: Open University Press.

NCSL (2004) *Gaining Tomorrow's School Leaders: The Challenge: Summary Report*. Nottingham: National College for School Leadership.

Stoll, L., Fink, D. and Earl, L. (2003) *It's About Learning (and it's About Time)*. London: RoutledgeFalmer.

Street, H. (2003) 'Editorial', *Secondary Leadership*. Paper Number 16. London: National Association of Headteachers.

Chapter 4

Staffing in Learning Schools

Preview

This chapter considers the following questions:

- **What will be the roles of teachers in ensuring effective learning?**
- **What roles will associate staff play in supporting the whole learning experience at school?**
- **How will students be supported in their emotional wellbeing?**
- **How will staffing be led and managed?**

> *A responsive and versatile, imaginative set of motivated professionals who can connect (learning) with young people in ways that make sense to them and in ways that expand their present view of reality.*
>
> Clarke (2000)

General principles

- As already noted, for all employees in a learning school the focus of what they do has to be on learning – the learning of students and their own. By staff in this chapter, we refer to anyone who is a paid employee of the school. Whatever job they do – teachers, assistants, technicians, resources manager, premises staff, office personnel, outreach workers etc – the work involved needs to be seen in relation to how learning is enhanced by what each individual does.
- In developing roles and tasks therefore, the key principle for leaders and managers is to begin with the support or development of learning that is needed and develop the jobs and roles from these, *not* the other way around.
- If all staff operate on this key principle, it becomes easier for learning schools to make a reality of what is a cliché of staff leadership and management in many schools i.e. valuing all staff equally. It is possible for schools to claim that all are valued equally but still, through daily practices and attitudes, display clear differences. In the learning school, there is an overt recognition that whatever tasks are carried out by an employee, they relate to the same

cause that one's own tasks are and therefore are important. All are interdependent. At the heart of this commitment will be the *relationships between the staff*.

Case example one

Swiss Cottage School in London has committed itself to a code of staff relationships which is constantly reviewed and updated. The policy states clearly that 'We review our performance against these guidelines annually'.

Swiss Cottage Staff Relationships Guidelines

Integrity is important in relationships – to help us achieve this, we have all agreed to consciously implement the following guidelines:

1. *Say it straight or you'll show it crooked – don't say one thing and think another.*
2. *Treat yourself and others with dignity and respect – remain professional at all times.*
3. *In a conflict, communicate only with those people who can help you resolve it. Talk directly and privately to the person you have a problem with – don't gossip.*
4. *Appropriately express your feelings in order to resolve the problem. Then you can get on with the tasks at hand.*
5. *Disentangle the issue from the person.*
6. *No moans, without defining the problem and looking for a possible solution – adopt a 'can do' approach.*
7. *Praise each other and celebrate individual and shared successes frequently.*
8. *Presume honourable motives – there usually is a good reason behind any decision. Remember that in the school context, decisions are always made in the best interests of our children.*
9. *Forgive and let go.*
10. *Greet each other with a word and a smile.*
11. *Join in, have fun and enjoy the company of your colleagues.*
12. *Make agreements that you intend and are able to keep.*
13. *In the face of difficulties, retain your sense of humour.*
14. *When under pressure, think before you act.*
15. *Recognise the stress colleagues may be under at times, and respond sensitively and appropriately.*

- The move to an emphasis on learning that is essentially personalised represents a massive shift in thinking and in practice away from conventional approaches. If it is to succeed, learning schools will need to utilise the skills and abilities of *all* stakeholders and lead learners associated with the school. This chapter therefore considers the roles of a number of these key people.

The role of teachers

Teaching-learning: learning-teaching

There is no doubt that teachers in twenty-first century learning schools will have to demonstrate great courage in lifting predetermined external pressures and liberating students from passive non-participation in the receiving, sifting and application of knowledge, in order that that knowledge leads to genuine understanding. McCall and Lawlor (2002 p.28) observe that:

> *Some people prefer to examine the hyphenated expression 'teaching-learning' or 'learning-teaching', rather than 'teaching' and 'learning' as apparently separate, if related entities. Certainly, some forms of classroom observation have been restricted in part by concentrating on what teachers 'do' as opposed to what students 'learn'. More recent lesson analysis does not treat teaching and learning as inputs and outputs, but as two sides of the same process.*

These observations lie at the heart, in our view, of what teachers will have to have at the forefront of their thinking, planning and preparation in new learning schools. Only relatively recently has the emphasis been much more firmly put on:

* how teachers can make students more proactive;
* how students can become an integral part of the teaching-learning process;
* how those being 'taught' can acquire the skills to be more effective learners.

Joyce et al (1999) develop this idea when describing what they call the 'evolutionary school':

> *The aspiration is to make all schools into learning communities for teachers as well as students, making best use of the best models for both... What we envision is a quantum leap toward the creation of a setting where inquiry is normal and the conditions of the workplace support the continuous, collegial inquiry that treats innovations as opportunities to study... where teaching and learning are examined continuously and improved in the course of engagement, where students are brought into the world of studying not only what they are learning in the 'curricular' sense, but their own situation and the progress they are making.*

Creating the learning culture: sharing the responsibility

Teachers will therefore have to be learners and vice versa. Creating a culture where learning is celebrated and practised by everyone who works in the organisation will make a significant difference: learning will not be seen as something to be *done*: rather it will be viewed as something to be *shared*. New learning schools will need to create a climate where positive working relationships operate within a shared ethos of enquiry and healthy critical debate. McCall and Lawlor (2002 p.31) suggest:

> *Students' relationships with their teachers and peers will in large degree be formed by the 'climate' in which learning takes place. In turn, this will arise from the educational values held, the level of expectation set, the conception of learning and how it should be managed, and the degree of shared responsibility for learning between teachers, students and the home.*

The matter of 'shared responsibility' is vitally important. The role of teachers in the current and anticipated context of sophisticated technology and access to almost unlimited knowledge streams means that they should and presumably will spend far less time imparting knowledge and far more time working with students in partnership to discover and unlock learning. E-learning alone, for example, presents significant and wholly new challenges. The changes and innovations we are already experiencing in how to improve teaching and learning carry with them quite dramatic implications:

- Conventional class sizes will almost certainly become a thing of the past. Teachers will work with groups of all sizes depending on the nature of the work, the needs of the learners and the relevant expertise of the subject staff.
- Robust home–school ICT links will revolutionise the established practice of 'going to school' to learn and inevitably change the way teachers currently operate.
- Webcams and video-conferencing are already impacting on learning and social groupings, not least because people are now able to see and talk to each other without needing to be in the same place.

Case example two

At Lent Rise Combined School, 8 and 9 year-olds linked up on four screens with children from four schools around the world – in France, Texas, Chicago and Brazil – and all the pupils practised their French together. Representatives from Hitachi have set up webcams in the school to establish links with a school in Japan. Last Christmas, a class of 4 year-olds met Santa Claus in Lapland thanks to video-conferencing.

Quoted in the *Times Educational Supplement* magazine *Teacher* p.12
28 November 2003

- Imaginative and well structured use by teachers of ICT will encourage students to become independent learners. Used intelligently, ICT will challenge the passive recipient of facts to become actively engaged in the learning.
- The new technologies will give students more control over their learning; by allowing them freedom to experiment and innovate, they will achieve greater independence and thus far more opportunities to personalise their learning.
- By making the school context less rigid and inflexible, teachers will be able to enter into much more imaginative and flexible contracts. There is no logical reason why in new learning schools, teachers should be restricted to one group of learners or one set of working hours: creating the 24-hour school will allow teachers the opportunity of working with a much wider and varied target audience where the emphasis is on developing learning, not just working through the formal school day with one age-restricted group of learners.

Case example three

A gifted science teacher living in the UK Midlands with an international reputation for using smartboard technology effectively in the classroom works part of the week in his school's science department, part of his time with professional consultancies and the rest (one day a week) as a freelance software producer. Often during his school holidays he travels to various destinations across the world (business class of course!) to run specialist workshops.

These observations do no more than hint at the tip of a demanding and potentially transformational iceberg. A recurrent theme in this book has been the fact that in an age where change is so rapid and complex, the major task facing teachers is to control and direct that change in part but always have at the centre of their thinking the central objective to empower the learner to take on the real responsibility for learning. Clarke (2000 p.9) notes:

... the established ways of teaching and learning will have to be redesigned because to learn about learning through experience and reflection cannot come from predefined, pre-planned curricula. These lessons come from a real connection with life beyond school, as well as within it, and they come from a responsive and versatile, imaginative set of motivated professionals who can connect such lessons with young people in ways that make sense to them and in ways that expand their present view of reality. Teachers have to be at the vanguard of change and reform, and they have to play an instructive role in creating the types of communities which can themselves learn.

It is an immense challenge but one nonetheless that teachers in twenty-first century schools will have to take on.

Developing the workforce

There seems to be little doubt that learning in schools will be delivered through entirely new networks of partnerships. The demands of the twenty-first century will impact on the structure and function of the educational workforce, both within schools and in the community. Hargreaves (2004 p.5) observes:

> It seems likely that, as the medical profession developed a considerable expansion of the para-medical professions during the twentieth century, the teaching profession will follow a similar line beyond the traditional technicians and teaching assistants of today. This enlargement of a more traditional workforce is crucial to personalisation.

The growing momentum in the UK over the last five years to redefine and heighten both the profile and the status of teaching assistants, for example, has not been a crude attempt to solve the teacher recruitment crisis. Rather, it has been an imaginative and innovative response to developing strategies which will address key issues surrounding the debate over how to make students more effective learners. Consider the following:

- new technologies are opening up tremendous opportunities to make learning exciting for the individual;
- many of those opportunities do not need teachers' direct input to make them happen;
- the national and indeed international shortage of teachers only exists if we cling to the traditional view that the only people who can make learning happen are 'properly qualified teachers';
- teaching assistants already play key roles in schools in leading learning: intelligent and targeted deployment of their knowledge and expertise can change and enhance the learning dynamic in the classroom;
- the concept of the 24-hour school accessed as a centre for learning for the local and wider community makes it inevitable that teachers will have to work with and alongside many other lead learners; they can't do it on their own!
- many other adults already take on learning roles in schools; deployed sensitively, their contribution must enhance and extend the role of the teacher;
- students, who are quite capable of making rational and intuitive choices about their educational needs, will play a much more central and proactive role in personalising their own learning.

Case example four

It is common practice for schools to use students on a rota basis to act as receptionists for visitors and at the same time to carry out tasks for the school office, such as taking messages, delivering goods etc. One girls' school in Torquay, Devon, however, related this quite specifically to the students' and office staff's learning.

At the end of their day of duty on reception, students were required to complete a learning log, stating what they felt they had learned from their work, both in factual terms about the job or school, and about themselves.

On a weekly basis, the ten students who had been involved met with the adult receptionist and either the PSHE co-ordinator or head of the relevant year or both for a 40 minute seminar on what they had all learned from doing the work – both students and adults – and how it related to their own learning, including in the formal curriculum.

Findings from these seminars were ultimately collated by the head of year, fed back to the office staff and the work of the student receptionist has been regularly modified in the light of these. By making the learning explicit, students were not tempted to see the job as either an escape from lessons or doing chores for the school.

For new partnerships to exist in the classroom, there needs to be a recognition that all those entrusted with developing student learning are working *with* each other, not *for* each other. New learning schools will not be able to foster a hierarchical outline where 'teachers' are regarded by definition as more qualified than others to lead learning; rather they will need to establish a climate where all those involved in the learning will use their particular skills to best effect. It is vital that these skills are seen as complementary. Middlewood and Parker (2001 p.202) suggest:

> The implications for leaders and managers in schools and colleges is that the starting point is not 'How can I make the teaching more effective here?' and providing assistance to the teacher, but rather 'How can learning be most effective here?' and providing a range of resources to enable this.

Staff in new learning schools will not be able to do this on their own. Politicians will need to realise that the freedom to innovate which this new millennium demands will only happen if government(s) take brave decisions and shift the emphasis away from directing how schools should operate to a culture based on genuine co-operation and shared objectives. Teachers will need to undertake roles and reach standards of practice quite unlike anything that has gone before. Prescriptive closed agendas for change set down in external directives by governments that have crude statistics-driven criteria for measuring success will not provide the experiences and the challenges this and subsequent generations of learners will need. McCall and Lawlor (2002 p.169) comment:

> *Any future standards of professional practice need to reflect exacting expectations about coping with diversity and uncertainty, but they must be set within a curriculum and professional development agenda that has vision, a strong sense of the 'teacher role' about objectives and strategies, and real commitment to offering effective learning to all.*

Teachers will continue to play a central role in new learning schools. However they will:

- be learners as well as teachers – for life;
- understand and accept that they are not the only means of delivering learning;
- work in partnership with other 'teachers' from the real and wider community;
- utilise and deploy the new technologies to best effect whenever possible;
- listen to the student voice;
- work alongside other staff in providing effective learning opportunities for all students.

None of this is especially revolutionary; indeed all of the above is already happening in a significant number of forward thinking schools. However, it needs to be the norm rather than the exception from now on if twenty-first century needs are going to be effectively met.

The role of staff in pastoral support

(a) Why support is needed

As various chapters in the book emphasise, along with all current thinking and research, emotional wellbeing is a crucial factor in effective learning. (See especially Goleman's work on emotional intelligence, 1996). For those committed to developing learning schools, it remains of high importance to remember that such inclusive schools have children and young people who have both uniquely individual circumstances and yet some common needs.

All pupils and students at the school are passing through important developmental stages of their lives, adolescence being an example of a period which usually brings high emotional turbulence. In addition, individuals may be handicapped by a whole range of factors, including:

- poor nutrition and/or hygiene at home and out of school;
- lack of balance in health factors such as lack of sleep, poverty and general deprivation;

- lack of emotional security at home;
- financial and 'caring for others' responsibilities;
- involvement with anti-social individuals or groups out of school;
- innate characteristics which single them out as 'different' in their out of school lives;

and many more.

Whilst being excited about prospects for new learning, its accessibility and its personalised potential, we recognise that each child and young person needs to learn in an environment which gives them the pastoral support they need as 'a person' as they progress through the development stages common to everyone (although clearly not all at the same time) and to help them where necessary mitigate some of the factors above which hinder their learning. Whilst schools cannot compensate for the deprivations and handicaps that some of its learners encounter, it can and should support them in two ways. The first is involving parents (see Chapter 11) and the community at large in its work and purpose. The second is by providing relevant staff support and structures within the learner's school environment.

(b) How support can be given

Traditionally secondary education in particular has been bedevilled by 'The Pastoral–Curriculum split' (Carnell and Lodge, 2002 p.113) with the subject teachers focusing on subject knowledge and tutor staff on personal issues, usually problems. Various attempts at restructuring to avoid this split have led to some new structures such as Year Learning Teams (Watkins, 1999) which deal with issues of both academic and pastoral relevance. These are important improvements and consciously constructed to make best use of school structures as they exist at present, but a focus on personalised learning requires much more flexibility, as mentioned, in groupings and needs to address the varied needs of learners at different times. As Carnell and Lodge (2002) point out, there has been very little written about the value of the work of pastoral staff in supporting young people's learning. They rightly advocate the bringing of:

> a varied range of experiences, skills and knowledge together in a holistic approach to the development and learning of the students.
>
> (ibid p.119).

We believe that the learning school has in its staffing as a whole precisely this varied range and that to restrict this supportive role to teachers is both inefficient use of teachers' time and a waste of the array of skills, experiences and knowledge elsewhere available in the school. The following example using the common tutorial system in English secondary schools illustrates what people apart from teachers can bring to this work.

Case example five

This large secondary community college in Leicestershire currently includes among its most effective tutors the following members of staff:

Name	Specialist job in school	Qualifications and experience
Brenda	Departmental Technician	Parent, employment in industry
Wendy	Librarian	Auntie, employment in local authority
Roger	IT Manager	Parent, self-employment, youth work, former driving instructor
Jane	Special Needs Assistant	Grandparent, employment in care homes and hospitals
Karen	Headteacher's PA	Auntie, member of local business group
Ian	Youth Worker	Elder brother, extensive travel, variety of jobs

Each has additionally the usual range of personal interests.
Duties include: the usual administrative tasks, checking on punctuality and attendance, discussing issues with students in their tutor groups, collectively and individually.

(c) Groupings

The model used in higher education may have much to offer, i.e. that each student has a personal tutor to whom they relate concerning their overall progress in learning and the factors that help or hinder this.

A school of 1,500 students is likely to have approximately 100 staff. It is possible therefore to envisage personal tutor groups of about 15 pupils or students, far more effective than more common sizes of 24 to 30.

Three things are required for the above:

- effective recruitment;
- effective training (both dealt with in the next section);
- a structured back-up specialist system to which tutors can refer either for discussing the student themselves or by referring the actual student.

Such specialist support may include:

- detailed help concerning entry to higher education;
- child psychologist;

- help with specific health and medical issues;
- help with certain social welfare concerns;
- police liaison.

If the school is 'at the heart of its community' and particularly as the 'one-stop' centre develops, most of these support services will be available on site.

Leadership and management issues in staffing

Those entrusted with the task of leading and managing twenty-first century schools will need to make bold decisions.

For example:

- The role of associate staff will develop significantly and impact on learning; there will be opposition – local, regional and national – to such arrangements and that opposition will have to be faced and overcome.
- In moving towards more flexible contracts, school leaders will have to risk financial loss in order to improve the quality of the provision.

Case example six

A UK secondary school in the Midlands has decided to appoint higher level teaching assistants to work in individual faculties. They will prepare and disseminate learning materials, take groups of students as and when appropriate and manage staff absence. Initially this will require considerable up front financial investment but the leadership group believe the initial investment will have significant mid/long-term benefits.

- Teachers will need to be convinced that their role is no longer confined to an audience made up of young people of compulsory school age. They will need to be encouraged and empowered by their leaders and managers to welcome the opportunity of working with learners of all ages.
- School leaders will need to ensure that attracting a much wider clientele to their school is welcomed as an opportunity and not seen as a threat.
- Those leading new learning schools will need to have at the centre of their staff recruitment and selection practices a determination to ensure that they will use imaginative and innovative strategies to meet the specific and wider needs of their learners.
- Bringing other teachers of learning into schools from, for example, the industrial, commercial and higher education sector will need to be managed sensitively and proactively in order to enhance the quality of what is on offer.

Training for the future

New learning schools will need to embrace and develop training as a key factor of their culture. In the UK, a relatively recent innovation has been the creation of a national network of Training Schools. These schools do not just provide training for a small number of new and/or aspiring teachers but rather set the training culture at the heart of their teaching and learning. Some of the strategies already in use in these schools might be regarded as radical. Some schools, for example, are already using students to give proactive informed evaluation of the quality of teaching and learning/curriculum delivery.

The evidence to date suggests strongly that by focusing on providing a range of programmes to deliver training, schools become:

- more reflective;
- more constructively critical;
- more adventurous;
- ultimately more effective.

Creating an ethos where calculated risk taking is encouraged within a no-blame culture will equip new learning schools to welcome and utilise revolutionary change. A recurrent theme in many of the chapters has been the recognition that the twenty-first century will require schools to operate in quite new ways; in order to do this they will need to have training and self-evaluation at the centre of their current and planned practice.

Staffing structures

Structures will be much less rigid than conventionally and, whilst there may well be role ambiguity for many, as Hall (1997 p.72) has pointed out:

> There is a positive side to role ambiguity. It is located in the space it allows for an individual to shape his or her own role.

Whilst schools focus on how to support and develop more and more personal-ised learning, they remain organisations with certain bureaucratic imperatives, e.g. recording attendance is likely to remain a statutory requirement. This means that the co-ordination of responsibilities will remain key and increasingly complex tasks for school leaders and managers. The implications of such contracts and roles as described in this chapter are returned to in Chapter 12.

Making the change

Positive learning environment

How do your staffing structures minimise or eliminate the pastoral–academic divide? How do they instead focus on meeting the needs of the students as priority?

- What steps have been taken to ensure that enquiry is seen as normal in the school?
- Do your documentation and observation processes focus on learning and teaching as a single two-way process and not on teaching as input and learning as output?
- What steps have been taken to move away from conventional school days? Continuous learning days? Staggered times for learning? Evenings as continuation of days?

Relationships

- Have you thought about devising through consensus a set of Staff Relationships Guidelines? How will you involve all employees?
- Do your contracts or contractual revision place sufficient emphasis on recognising the personal and professional needs of staff?
- If certain colleagues have opportunities for a number of days out of school per year, have you considered approaching their contracts from a different standpoint, i.e. start with the days as given, and devise a contract by which both school and the individual benefit – including financially – removing potential guilt and resentment from the situation?

Case example seven

A long serving head of PE department in a large community college with day and evening classes wanted to spend more time at home with his children. His wife wanted to increase her part-time commitment from two to three days a week at the same college. The solution was to offer the head of PE a new role – Director of Community Sport – and a much more flexible contract. This included three days a week when he began teaching at 2.00pm and finished at 9.00 pm after taking a range of evening classes and managing the physical education programme. This meant he could spend more time at home with his children and his wife could increase her work commitment. They gained financially, domestically and professionally from the arrangement, and the college had two more fulfilled employees.

Emotional intelligence

- What steps have been taken to ensure that teachers do not see the development of, for example, teaching assistants' roles as a threat to their own status? Have you tried to indicate – through skills workshops, for example – how the work of assistants in taking over reasonably high level tasks enables the status of teachers to be actually upgraded not downgraded?
- Have staff audits of stress factors been carried out and have they been engaged with in strategies to deal with these? Have you ensured that *all* staff's stress factors were included in these?

- What strategies/rituals have developed in the school for recognising staff achievements?

Engagement

- Have you considered using staff other than teachers as personal tutors for students? What training needs to be provided?
- Has there recently been an audit of all staff talents so that deployment can be based as much as possible upon these?
- Does training and development take account of the range of learning styles existing in the people or teams concerned?

References

Carnell, E. and Lodge, C. (2002) *Supporting Effective Learning*. London: Paul Chapman.

Clarke, P. (2000) *Learning Schools, Learning Systems*. London: Continuum.

Goleman, D. (1996) *Emotional Intelligence*. London: Bloomsbury.

Hargreaves, D. (2004) *Personalising Learning: Next steps in Working Laterally*. London: Specialist Schools Trust.

Hall, V. (1997) 'Management roles in education' in T. Bush and D. Middlewood (eds) *Managing People in Education*. London: Paul Chapman.

Joyce, B., Calhoun, E. and Hopkins, D. (1999) *The New Structure of School Improvement: Inquiring Schools and Achieving Students*. Oxford: Oxford University Press.

McCall, C. and Lawlor, H. (2002) *Leading and Managing Effective Learning*. London: Optimus.

Middlewood, D. and Parker, R. (2001) 'Managing curriculum support staff for effective learning' in D. Middlewood and N. Burton (eds) *Managing the Curriculum*. London: Paul Chapman.

Watkins, C. (1999) 'The case for restructuring the UK secondary school pastoral care' in *Education*, Vol. 17 no. 4 pp. 3–10.

Chapter 5

Teachers As Learners

Preview

This chapter considers the following questions:

- Why is it important for teachers to understand the way they learn?
- What training and support do teachers and other staff need to facilitate optimum learning for students?
- How can research-based practice impact on the learning and attainment of students?
- What part do mentors and informal networking play in teachers' learning and classroom pedagogy?
- How can we create the culture of reflective practice and lifelong learning in our staffrooms?

> *The reflective learning school is one where all who aid learning are willing to adapt their teaching constantly until it works. We have yet to fully understand the magic of the inner brain.*
>
> John MacBeath

Context

The national reforms in many countries during the 1990s increased competition between schools. In this context, professional development was seen to be vital in securing school improvement. Recent research has indeed shown that professional development is an essential part of improving school performance (Bolam, 2002). Hence 'teachers as learners' is a fundamental concept under-pinning the ethos and practice in the learning school for the twenty-first century. However, the definition of 'teacher' and that of 'professional development' may need redefining in the context of the twenty-first century learning school.

- teachers are not only qualified classroom practitioners but any adult engaged in helping young people learn and make progress (hence the title of this chapter refers to 'teachers' in this sense);

- professional development is an ongoing self-activated process of reflection and review that dovetails with performance management and engages with the needs of the individual and the school;
- learning is a process of self-development that results in personal growth as well as development of skills and knowledge that facilitate the education of young people.

This paradigm moves professional development away from the practice of attending courses and training days to the concept of lifelong learning as being part of the entitlement and obligation of all staff within a school. As Bush and Middlewood (2005) suggest:

> a school or college which is able to encourage its teachers, support staff and ideally all its employees to learn and continue to learn should be the one that is most effective in helping its pupils or students learn.

Chapter 4 considered how new forms of staffing can be used to support optimum learning within the school. This chapter will focus on what can be done to ensure that the culture of the school reflects a desire to make everyone in it a learner, reflecting upon their practice, thereby creating an energy which permeates the whole school community.

The concept of a 'learning organisation' originated in the business world as a response to the need for change and growth. Those schools that have embraced this notion have found it a key to their success through:

- providing a focus on learning;
- regarding needs of the learner as central;
- establishing an ethos of enquiry;
- recognising that learning comes from many sources;
- acknowledging that learning is a lifelong process and that the school is making a contribution to this;
- schools accepting that they need to be in a constantly transformational state.

This can cause tensions amongst staff who yearn for stability and routine. Dale (1994 p. 4) suggests that the ideal state for staff being one where 'learning and working are actually synonymous.' This could be seen as a mirror image of the experience of a child in school who needs to view all experience as learning and needs time to reflect on how to move forward. The first step of every learning experience is to understand where you are now.

Teachers understanding the way they learn

> Education (is) at the centre of public policy with the core task of helping people transform how they think of themselves.
>
> (Desforges, 1999)

As you read this, are you sipping a coffee or munching a chocolate bar? Is there music on or do you need silence? Can you work late at night or do you prefer the early hours? How about your desk – tidy and organised or a mound of paper, cigarette butts and dirty coffee cups? It matters. We all learn differently and we all need to find what works for us. In Chapters 7 and 8, the focus is on how to understand students as individual learners. The same principle applies to teachers.

It is vital that teachers reflect on their learning style because it will impact on their teaching style and this will in turn impact on their success or failure in the classroom. A teacher's learning style will have a direct impact on the way he or she teaches. This will affect some students more than others. For example a teacher who is a highly visual learner will question students using phrases like 'Can you see it?', 'Do you know what I am looking for?', will speak very quickly and use lots of visual devices to teach. For some students this will be highly effective, for others it will not. Some teachers love to engage in role play and group work whereas others will feel less in control and will need support for this type of activity. These teacher preferences can impact on the behaviour, attitude and progress of whole classes. They can also impact on the attitude and progress of our own staff learners. As Svinicki (1996), researching at the Center for Teacher Effectiveness, stated:

> we need to be as diverse and flexible in our teaching about teaching as we expect faculties to be in their teaching about content.

Understanding the impact of teachers' own personal preferences and learning styles can be used to advantage in planning the timetable and curriculum.

Case example one

The behaviour and attitude of a Year 7 class was causing concern to a secondary school in the south of England. It had deteriorated during the course of the year and now had a reputation for being the worst class in the year group. By paying careful attention to students' learning profiles and matching them with kinaesthetic teacher profiles (i.e. those that enjoyed role play and practical activity) the timetable of this class was carefully planned for Year 8. The outcome was very positive – the form went from the worst to the best behaved class in the year group as their learning needs were matched with their teachers' styles of delivery.

Nurturing self-awareness in the learning school

The following are important factors to consider which influence staff learning. Adults may:

- bring a wide range of previous knowledge and skills to learning;
- feel anxiety and fear of judgement in coming to new learning;
- resist what they believe is an attack on their competence;
- need to see results of their learning and to have accurate feedback.

(Adapted from Brookfield, 1986)

In many schools, some teaching staff have been in post doing things 'their way' for a number of years and, as Taylor and Bishop (1994) point out, 'unlearning' is extremely difficult. The opportunity presented by the new learning styles agenda outlined above offers a new way for teachers to reflect on themselves and by extension on their practice. The Assessment for Learning paradigm (see Chapter 8) gives a context for teaching staff to measure their success in achieving progress for students. There is an opportunity to help teachers grow personally and professionally through educating them about the impact on learning of discoveries in neuroscience and intelligence.

The reflective learning school is one where teachers are willing to adapt their teaching constantly until it works.

As stated above, all teaching staff in schools need to examine their own learning styles to help them reflect upon their natural teaching style.

A simple brain hemisphere test (see Chapter 7) will help teachers understand their tendency towards creative or systematic thinking and a test for visual, auditory or kinaesthetic preferences will demonstrate how natural inclinations can lead directly into classroom practice. It is our experience that when teachers discover their own learning styles they become more sensitive and reflective about students' styles of learning and more willing to adapt their teaching or planning to provide an inclusive approach. Indeed, one teacher who undertook some learning styles analysis examined the conclusions and stated 'now I understand why I struggled in school and always do spider diagrams when I am trying to understand or plan something important.'

To this audit of teacher learning styles can be added a reflection on teachers' perception of their emotional intelligence. As outlined by Goleman (1996) these include empathy, optimism, persistence, mood control, deferred gratification, goal setting, stress management and self-esteem.

In a later work, Goleman (1998) talks of people who have initiative and optimism as ready to:

- seize opportunities;
- pursue goals beyond what is required or expected of them;
- cut through the red tape and bend rules when necessary to get the job done;

- mobilise others through unusual, enterprising efforts;
- persist in seeking goals despite obstacles and setbacks;
- operate from hope of success rather than fear of failure;
- see setback as due to manageable circumstance rather than a personal flaw.

Such qualities are essential for good learners, be they students or staff. If we wish to nurture emotional intelligence in students, it is vital that teachers model it. As de Andres (1999) points out, teachers' responses 'serve as mirrors through which children see and judge their image.' Hence emotional intelligence in the teaching staff is a crucial layer within the hierarchy of needs for the learning school for twenty-first century.

> Mistakes are turned to advantage as learning opportunities since learners with high self-esteem are not worried about giving the wrong answers or appearing stupid in front of their classmates.
>
> (Head, 1996)

So it is with teachers too. Teachers need be confident and not afraid to make mistakes. When self-esteem is high the ability to accept advice and feedback leads to positive progress. The ongoing process of continuous learning is a risky business that takes courage and support. As Svinicki (1996) found:

> Becoming a learner again means exposing oneself to the possibility of failure, an unpleasant prospect to anyone accustomed to being knowledgeable and in charge.

Truly reflective practice in school means regular self-evaluation and that means asking students what they think of your teaching.

The HayMcBer Transfoming Learning questionnaire provides a tool that tests out the climate of the classroom by asking students to make direct judgements about perceptions of their teachers fairness, expertise and ability to communicate. Teachers who have taken part in this find it daunting but very interesting. 'I didn't know they felt I had favourites' was one teacher's feedback. But it is crucial to know what students think and reflection is more forcefully on the legislative performance agenda than ever before in the UK through parents' and students' questionnaires under the 2004 framework for school inspection.

Figure 5.1 *Luft's model of the Johari Window (1969).*

	Known to self	Not known to self
Known to others	OPEN	BLIND
Not known to others	HIDDEN	UNKNOWN

The Johari window model (see Figure 5.1) helps one understand that self-disclosure leads to self-knowledge and therefore self-awareness – an essential component of learning. Teachers who become truly self-aware then have the ability to develop meaningful targets. Schools can also model this self-reflection by regularly canvassing the attitudes of parents and students towards school. As the OPEN section of the model in Figure 5.1 expands so self-awareness increases. When you know more about yourself you can continue to develop and learn.

A safe environment in which to share mistakes and triumphs is an essential part of the learning school. Formal and informal opportunities for such reflection, for example at team meetings, or chatting in the staffroom to a mentor or passing colleague, will promote emotional intelligence.

> *You cannot raise the self-esteem of someone else above the level of your own.*
>
> Ian Gilbert 2002

There are some strategies which can enhance the self-reflection necessary to create the emotionally intelligent staffroom:

- a learning news board with varied populist and academic learning stories for sharing;
- a learning newsletter in which teachers share successes and failures;
- a learning group where teachers discuss innovation and volunteer to try out new thinking on classroom practice and share the outcomes in the group and then with the whole staff;
- a learning journal kept by all staff;
- feedback to teachers from students through Transforming Learning or in registration/questionnaires;
- displaying posters and peripheral learning slogans such as 'Every mistake is a learning experience';
- praise and reward for staff – nominate staff for a bottle of wine every week;
- honest accountability of leaders 'I got it wrong ...';
- research-based practice as a norm;
- a development and research culture – development followed by research.

By acknowledging more fully the learner in ourselves at all levels of school organisation, the context for true staff development can be developed. In addition we need to acknowledge the wide range of opportunities for learning within the context of a school environment. (see Figure 5.2)

Coaching, mentoring and empowering

'Mentoring has become one of the cults of the age,' said Margaret Wilkin of Homerton College, Cambridge. Schools and other organisations are using mentors 'to induct and advise newcomers in a new social trend' where the

Figure 5.2 *Opportunities for learning in the school context*

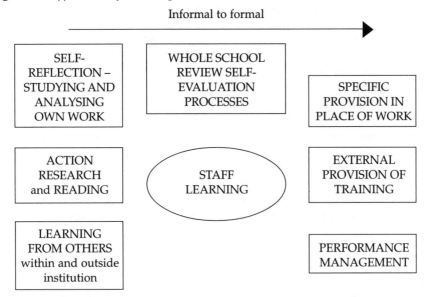

external pressures of change demand a rapid change in performance from staff new to the company or new to their role. As Clutterbuck (1991) puts it 'with the help of the mentor, the protégé assesses himself and discovers where his skills, aspirations and interests lie.' Conway (1994) suggests there is a powerful relationship between mentoring and creativity. In schools the mentor needs to balance support and encouragement with the demands for development. In the reflective twenty-first century learning school the 'critical friend' who provides an opportunity to open the window (see Figure 5.1) to self-knowledge and self-awareness, in a non-threatening informal context, is an invaluable asset to staff development.

> *Being a mentor offers the chance to learn about yourself as you support someone else to grow. It is a powerful learning experience that stays with you longer than any course or INSET day.*
>
> (Teacher in a London secondary school)

Mentoring may consist of:

- introducing staff to the people and systems that matter in the school;
- regular meetings in the staff room to share experience;
- comparing lesson plans and experiences with similar classes or pupils;
- keeping learning diaries to share highs and lows;
- advising about professional development opportunities or areas of concerns regarding contracts or working conditions;

- sharing resources;
- sharing the way 'we do things round here.'

As mentoring progresses to a more coaching role, it may include:

- mutual lesson observation with feedback sessions;
- target setting and monitoring;
- videoing each others' lessons to discuss pedagogy;
- teaching each others' classes or team teaching as appropriate;
- joint activities such as visits, trips or leading an INSET session for other staff.

An extension of this approach is to create 'buddies' within or across departments, schools or phases. This takes time and organisation but can be tremendously beneficial. Even for staff close to capability procedures, it may be easier to set up a buddy system than go through formal processes.

Case example two

A science department in the Midlands had two members who were struggling for different reasons. One with general pedagogy and reaching the right level for students at KS3 and the other with discipline and classroom management. These teachers were 'buddied' with members of the department who were strongest on these skills and capabilities. The outcome was a non-threatening opportunity for these members of staff to review their performance with a critical friend, the 'buddy', and set targets for improvement. Over a period of two terms improvements were seen and this process was recorded as part of training needs in performance management documentation.

An extension of this type of work is the development of a new type of teacher promoted to spread good practice through outreach work. The Advanced Skills Teacher (AST) or lead practitioner is assessed as 'expert' and given time and money to specialise in excellent classroom practice that can be modelled and shared with other teachers in their own schools and others. In England this appears to have been a very successful initiative with 4,000 teachers advising and supporting others across England. They work with staff sharing good practice and modelling pedagogy with students as an alternative to choosing the strategic leadership option for career development. The strength of this approach is the way it has shifted the financial and hierarchical rewards for those involved away from administrative tasks and towards learning. Leading learning has become an opportunity for promotion, with many Advanced Skills Teachers also sitting on the Senior Leadership Team influencing strategic planning.

For coaching and mentoring to succeed, the chemistry between the relevant staff has to be right so the systems need to allow opportunities for change and flexibility. The purpose of this section is to provide some ideas of how mentoring and coaching at all levels can provide the structure for the reflective practice that will be an essential part of the learning school for the twenty-first century.

Teachers as researchers

In 1930 John Dewey, the great American education thinker, said 'teachers' potential contribution to research is an "unworked mine".' With 5,000 teachers becoming involved in Best Practice Research Scholarships in the UK and a renewed interest in the international dimension to research, has the mine begun to be worked?

Many schools are actively engaged in promoting an active research culture in the school. This can be developed through developing a culture of enquiry and reflection. Day (1999) argues for schools to be 'communities of reflective practice' so that staff can share wisdom and mistakes. To develop this reflective culture Vaill (1989) advocates the Chinese concept of Wu-wei – the art of non-action. He says this is about learning to go with the flow, or follow the grain. Bush and Middlewood (2005) state that this does not 'counsel passivity' but a focus more on the 'how and why' rather than the 'what'. This is in line with our encouragement of students to engage in metacognition – stand back and think about how and why you are thinking like that … As they conclude:

> the more people discovered about their own learning and the complex nature of learning itself, the more they needed to share this with others and thus move from the intuitive to the explicit in terms of normal staff practice.

However, more action-based research can provide an opportunity for staff at all levels within the organisation to provide information and action plans in their own area of interest so it is a very empowering concept. It also underpins the whole ethos of the learning school environment where everyone is engaged in reflective practice and considers themselves to be a learner.

Case example three

A primary school in Solihull decided to trial an Exercise for Learning programme which aimed to help students gain more self-discipline and control by physical exercises. The students were selected and a control group identified. Nine months on and the research group had made marked progress and were 14 months ahead on reading and comprehension compared to eight months' progress of the control group.

A teacher involved in the research said 'it's such a change from being on the receiving end of initiatives imposed from the outside.' Now this school is extending its project to help more students.

Case example four

A large secondary school in Milton Keynes took the opportunity to review its professional development when it increased its total numbers by adding an extra year's intake. In an effort to engage staff in research on teaching and learning, the school worked with the Open University to form a staff group studying for an MA module. Ten per cent of the staff are attending the course and one teacher was asked what impact it had had on the classroom practice:

> *I used to label the students high or low ability. But now I'm much more wary about the whole concept of innate intelligence. I use praise as a motivating tool much more and have changed the way I use language.*
>
> *(Times Educational Supplement, July 2004)*

Case example five

As already mentioned in Chapter 3, the National College for School Leadership runs a Research Associates' programme to encourage evidence based practice. A teacher at a Nottinghamshire secondary school decided to research the changing role of middle leaders as part of the research associates programme, with 30 days spread over three terms to complete the study. The research is prompted by an acknowledgement of the way expectations made of middle pastoral and curriculum leaders have changed and a desire to quantify the impact of these changes. The research will include interviews and working diaries, minutes of meetings and job descriptions and a comparison with focus groups from other schools. It is designed to provide career progression and benefit schools and colleges where the researcher can feed back the outcomes. In addition, the teacher becomes skilled in research methodology and aware of how her own students feel when faced with a struggle to meet deadlines!

Ensuring all staff have access to continuing professional development

Chapter 4 illustrated how staffing the learning school will involve many more varied roles than the traditional teacher and Learning Support Assistant. A flexible approach to adults working with children means that all staff may work with and teach children and help create the learning culture. From the receptionist training a student on community service for the day to a lunchtime supervisor resolving a playground quarrel to the caretaker who also teaches self-defence in his lunchtime (see case study below) – *all* our staff should be role models in lifelong learning. This means all staff must be equally valued as Middlewood (2005) reflects:

- Do all staff have equal access to the staffroom?
- Do staff lists reflect hierarchies?
- Do staff photographs include all staff?
- Are staff and school events open to all staff?
- Are the achievements of support staff valued and recognised in the same way as those of teachers?

In addition, are the support staff receiving their full entitlement to appraisal and staff development training opportunities? There is much untapped talent on the support staff of any school and the learning school needs to make sure it is nurtured and used for the benefit of the students.

Case example six

In a Northamptonshire school it was discovered that the school caretaker was a qualified and experienced karate and self-defence coach. His services were then used during family learning days, PE and lunchtime classes to teach on the Instructors scale for students of all ages. This was enjoyed by students and enhanced the culture of all staff as teachers and learners. He is now training to become a Higher Level Teaching Assistant.

At the same school, when it was realised that the IT technician had a degree in ICT she was assessed and accepted for graduate teacher training. She now combines both roles in order to sustain her income before she qualifies as a teacher.

Tapping into the potential of all is a crucial aspect of the twenty-first century learning school. A paper from the National College for School Leadership suggested that schools should be 'listing' potential candidates for school roles well before the posts are vacant, in order to provide training and experience in advance. This is particularly useful for posts harder to fill such as pastoral roles. By 'listing' potential candidates staff can be encouraged to work with pastoral leaders in a mentoring/coaching role and discover whether or not this role will suit their skills and attributes. It also facilitates professional development and career progression even in staffrooms where opportunities don't come up very frequently because there is little movement of staff.

Collaborative networks

No one person can educate a child in the modern context. The pedagogic knowledge necessary is spread across a number of minds... Networks provide a direct mechanism for knowledge transfer.'

(Desforges, 2004)

More and more schools are finding it beneficial to share resources and expertise in order to move forward on issues relating to student achievement. This is having an impact on teacher learning where teachers take themselves out of their own context and examine similar problems in a different organisation. This is one of the most powerful agents of change for our learning school because where a teacher may be considered set in their ways and reluctant to change in their own setting they can suddenly see themselves in a different light when working with colleagues from another institution.

Where collaboratives have been set up they have brought subject leaders together to find ways to make a difference and raise standards. In England the collaboratives have often involved underachieving schools working with high attaining schools. In the electronic age schools have been able to break down the barriers of time and distance and collaborate through video conferencing and e-mail. Where these groups are set up in an open and emotionally intelligent context, the learning is synergistic and a powerful agent for change. These collaboratives aren't just about sharing resources and cultures – they are fundamental to an open minded and reflective approach to 'the way we do things round here'. They can involve mutual observations, staff exchanges, joint recruitment and joint training events. Where competition is replaced with collaboration, mutual learning is a certainty and therefore a prerequisite for twenty-first century learning schools.

Case example seven

A head of faculty in Sussex had been in position for 15 years and was feeling rather stale and drained, with subject results declining and pressure to improve performance from management. When she was asked to join and help lead a collaborative group via an Excellence in Cities partnership it seemed like one more meeting but a year on the benefits have been enormous. It has given her confidence in the strengths of her programme at Key Stage Four and the resources and ideas she could share with others for raising their grades. She has shared mutual observation at Key Stage Three and planned new schemes of work as an outcome. Her enthusiasm for the subject has been replenished by discussions with other colleagues outside her own department and plans are afoot to share some teaching via video conferencing.

Can performance management make an impact on learning?

Regardless of which particular system of official performance management is in place in schools, it will include observation and feedback and target setting. It is in the target setting that we can make a difference to the focus for school development.

Current guidelines for performance management in the UK state clearly that at least one objective must relate to learning and innovative practice, one to assessment for learning and one to personal development. Thus there is a clear rationale to the process of performance management and how it relates to the development of the learning school ethos.

Using a whole school review process

Another method in the learning school is to use **whole school review** as a self-reflective tool for developing whole school learning. This process consists of self-assessment of all aspects of school work, including departments and working groups against agreed criteria. Each group will use a questionnaire to self reflect then a number of other measures to triangulate this evidence. Lesson observation, scrutiny of work, student voice input, observing meetings and a handbook should form part of the process. The report is led by a member of the senior leadership team and written up as a report that is presented to school governors in the presence of the team leader. The process reflects the measures used when schools are externally audited so provides a self-evaluation tool so that action can be taken to identify issues or areas for development.

Can we measure how effective staff learning is?

How can we judge the effectiveness of the professional development culture within the school setting? Bush and Middlewood (2005) suggest some key indicators of progress may be:

- Are meetings centred on debate rather than administrative issues?
- Are more staff using the libraries and resources centre?
- Are more staff offering to lead discussions?
- Are staff acknowledging the role of other agents in the learning role e.g. parents?
- Are staff willing to identify and acknowledge mistakes (their own and others) as learning experiences?
- Are the barriers to creativity in learning and teaching being recognised?
- Are the learning capabilities of all staff being recognised and acted upon?
- Are the different learning styles for staff being recognised in learning?
- Are all staff having opportunities to formalise their learning achievements, if they wish to do so, and what proportion are doing so?

We would add a measure of staff seeking promotions within and outside the school, research and writing projects staff may be involved in, and staff participation in various self-evaluation exercises including whole school review or questionnaires with students or parents to get feedback on performance.

Transforming learning, transforming minds

Some of the above suggestions are already part of practice in continuing professional development in schools, although very few have a systematic approach to seeing it as a whole. In order to create learning institutions that prepare our youngsters for the twenty-first century there may be another weapon in our learning armoury that will help teachers to become learners for life – NLP.

Neuro-linguistic programming is often termed 'the user's manual for the mind' and one of the authors (Beere) as a practitioner of NLP is an ardent advocate of its application to create real transformation in learning for teacher and students. It is based on the work of Bandler and Grinder (1979) and encompasses a whole range of techniques for using language to create change and growth. It is based on some important underlying principles that are useful as benchmarks in any staffroom culture:

- there is no such thing as failure, only feedback;
- we all have all the resources we need to do whatever we want to;
- all behaviour has a positive intention;
- the meaning of your communication is the response it gets;
- if it doesn't work try something else, if that doesn't work try something else, if that doesn't work try something else and if that doesn't work try something else etc. ... until it *does* work!

It has been said that using NLP strategies is the way to create emotional intelligence because it enables you to manage your fears and self-doubt by replacing them with new psychological programmes of hope. The detail and explanation for these strategies used in education are clearly beyond the scope of this chapter.

One echo of NLP thinking that would permeate every 21st century learning school's continuing professional development ethos would be the simple truth.

Be the change you want to see.

Ghandi

Making the change

Creating the positive learning environment

- provide resources for formal and informal learning, ranging from a daily newspaper to the latest pedagogical theory texts;
- create an interactive website and intranet that can be used as a learning tool for teachers as well as students;
- have a 'learning' noticeboard and newsletter to share good practice informally;
- make sure staff training events are at quality venues with a high standard of refreshments and resources to make staff feel training is valued;
- encourage an ongoing informal debate about learning in 'open-door' staffrooms and classrooms;
- ensure hierarchies in school reflect a focus on learning as a priority rather than management tasks;

- make sure performance management systems include objectives related to assessment for learning, engagement with learning and self-learning;
- express clearly the values of lifelong learning through posters and display.

Relationships

- encourage frequent sharing of experiences in the classroom – both good and bad;
- use outreach work at other schools as a means of bringing learning back into the school through staff such as ASTs leading training events;
- establish a system for mentoring, buddying and coaching;
- keep staff morale high by making special awards on a regular basis; these can include the trivial – laughing in the staffroom should be encouraged!
- give clear tips on promoting good working relationships with ALL staff in school policies and handbooks;
- celebrate achievement, academic and otherwise in staff briefings.

Emotionally intelligent schools

- train staff to understand the importance of emotional intelligence – include a test on their own EQ;
- include emotional intelligence indicators in performance management criteria. For example, encourage an aspirational target for student achievement to be to encourage an optimistic approach. Encourage staff who find relationships with students confrontational, to do the Hay McBer Transforming Learning classroom ethos test with their students;
- establish a system of whole school review where every department and group within school undertakes a regular self-reflection exercise to evaluate their performance and set up an action plan;
- investigate NLP as a tool for transforming learning.

Engagement using learning styles

- encourage all staff to undertake a learning styles self-assessment in order to discover more about their way of learning;
- make sure training is offered in ways that will tap into the strengths and preferences of all staff;
- involve as many staff as possible in planning training and encourage interactive approaches.

Reflective learning

- encourage research-based practice through personal interest projects, higher degree courses or participation in national research projects;
- encourage innovation and risk taking in pedagogy and all aspects of school life;
- Ensure that there are planned opportunities for staff to feed back what they have learned to each other.

References

De Andres (1999) 'Self-Esteem in the classroom or the metamorphosis of butterflies' in J. Arnold (ed) *Affect in Language Learning*. Cambridge: Cambridge University Press.

Bandler, R. and Grinder, J. (1979) *Frogs into Princes*. New York: Real People Press.

Bolam (2002) *'Professional Development and Professionalism'* in T. Bush and L. Bell (eds) *The Principles and Practice of Educational Management*. London: Paul Chapman.

Brookfield, S. (1986) *Understanding and Facilitating Adult Learning*. Milton Keynes: Open University Press.

Bush, T. and Middlewood, D. (2005) *Leading and Managing People in Education*. London: Paul Chapman.

Clutterbuck, D. (1991) *Everyone Needs a Mentor*. Wimbledon: Institute of Personnel Management.

Conway, C. (1994) *Mentoring Managers in Organisations:* Berkhamsted: Ashridge.

Dale, M. (1994) 'Learning organisations' in C. Mabey and P. Iles (eds) *Managing Learning*. London: Routledge.

Day, C. (1999) 'Professional learning communities', in H. Busher and R. Saran (eds) *Managing Teachers as Professionals in Schools*. London: Kogan Page.

Desforges, C. (1999) *Learning, Routledge International Companion to Education*. London: Routledge.

Desforges, C. (2004) 'Collaboration for transformation' in *Nexus*. National College for School Leadership Networked Learning Communities Publication.

Gilbert, I. (2002) *Essential Motivation in the Classroom*, London: RoutledgeFalmer.

Goleman, D. (1996) *Emotional Intelligence*. London: Bloomsbury.

Goleman, D. (1998) *Working with Emotional Intelligence*. London: Bloomsbury.

Head, K. (1997) *Self-esteem for Teachers and Learners*. Cambridge: Heinemann.

Middlewood, D. (2005) 'Leading and managing staff and organisational learning' in T. Bush and D. Middlewood (eds) *Leading and Managing People in Education*. London: Sage.

Svinicki, M. (1996) *When Teachers become Learners*. Center for Teacher Effectiveness: University of Texas.

Taylor, D. and Bishop, S. (1994) *Ready Made Activities for Developing Your Staff*. London: Pitman.

Wilkin, M., Everton, T. and Younger, M. (1997) *Report on the Effects of School-based Training on Secondary Schools*, Cambridge: Homerton College.

Vaill, P. (1989) *Managing as a Performing Art: New Idea for a World of Chaotic Change*. San Francisco: Jossey-Bass.

Chapter 6

Resourcing the Learning Environment

Preview

This chapter considers the following questions:

- How can we build world class schools of the future which will cater for and anticipate entirely new consumer demands?
- How do we successfully manage the move away from the current school day/school year to take advantage of the economic and global opportunities presented by the concept of the 24-hour school?
- How can we harness, deploy and make best use of modern technologies to enhance the quality of teaching and learning in the twenty-first century school?
- How can we ensure that all those stakeholders with a proven ability to deliver effective teaching and learning are best deployed to provide the quality and variety of educational provision required in new learning schools?

> *If one allowed for varying degrees of artifice and architecture, school buildings tend to look the same the world over.*
>
> Beare (2001)

No reason to change?

For much of the last century schools, in spite of everything going on around them in terms of change and development, stubbornly remained to all intents and purposes unchanged. In fact, up until a few years ago there was a great deal of perceived wisdom in the observation that if a Victorian surgeon walked in to a modern operating theatre he would be overwhelmed but if a Victorian teacher entered a modern classroom he could begin teaching. Beare (2001 p.1) comments:

> *For the whole twentieth century at least, the school took children at 5 or 6, put them into class groups composed of children of the same age and allocated students and teachers to a self contained classroom. There the pupils were led through a*

curriculum based on the notion that human knowledge is divided into 'subjects'.

Unsurprisingly perhaps, even the actual school buildings have not changed radically. Traditionally they have been:

- of similar design;
- set in similar contexts;
- built on the notion that learning could be distinctive, coherent and managed.

Again, Beare (2001 p.1), in an expansion of this chapter's opening quote notes:

The formal instruction is conducted in sets of relatively large buildings consisting of rows of classrooms spinning into big passageways which are designed to control or at least co-ordinate student movement. If one allowed for varying degrees of artifice and architecture, school buildings tend to look the same the world over.

Opportunity, flexibility: blurring the boundary edges

Schools can no longer be designed to deliver a restricted and heavily directed curriculum. They must have as a central objective the opportunity and flexibility to offer learning routes for a much wider potential market than just the current 3–18 student population. They must become centres for learning and be flexible and imaginative resources accessed by all those who are genuinely interested in and excited by the possibility of extending their educational horizons. Schools in the twenty-first century will be:

- open more often than they are closed;
- accessed by the local, regional, national and global community;
- designed in such a way to allow flexibility of access and curriculum delivery.

Hargreaves (1997 p.4) makes a fundamentally important observation about future schooling:

*I believe it will become more difficult over the next twenty five years to talk about 'the education system' in the sense of a distinctive, coherent and managed system ... The traditional 'education system' must be replaced by a **polymorphic** educational provision – an infinite variety of multiple forms of teaching and learning.*

There is plenty of evidence already that the leading schools in the UK and other developed countries are already global, building as they do links with overseas providers of learning. Schools are emerging which are offering:

- full service school centres bringing together welfare and community develop-

ment agencies;
• a wide range of out of hours learning opportunities for people of all ages from all backgrounds.

In this way, the local established traditional setting of clear boundary lines between the school and the community are becoming increasingly difficult to define, a point stressed by Beare (2001 p.189):

Schooling becomes education of the community in the community and largely by the community ... they are spoken of as a service or a process rather than a geographical location, a campus.

Radical innovation: future schools

In 1995 a report by the Organisation for Economic Co-operation and Development raised four fundamental considerations in attempting to rationalise how schools of the future will look:

1. *Defining the place for learning*: will new models for learning develop and how will the classroom of the future look?
2. *Building connections*: will the traditional building be influenced by the networking power of new technologies? How much physical space will we actually need?
3. *New building use requirement*: will information technology open schools up to significantly larger and more diverse populations? Will such increased open access trigger entirely new approaches to building design?
4. *Transforming support facilities for learning*: how will we address the massive demands implicit in the dissemination, maintenance and support of increasingly complex information technology to a much broader client base?

These questions are asking us to consider how schools:

• can build into their design the capacity to take on the new technologies;
• deal with the increased demands of a society that needs to keep up to date and up-skill on a regular basis just to stay afloat;
• take into consideration the fact that much of their client base will have the technology to access learning from home or at work.

All of these factors once again point to the necessity for schools to be flexible, adaptable and multi-functional.

Building schools for the future

Nearly 20 years ago, the challenge was being laid down by those suggesting that education was bursting out of the schooling system. They saw school as a feudal industrial concept, and as obsolete and unworkable.

The consultation document Building Schools for the Future (DfES, 2003) made the UK government's key objective clear:

> *Local education authorities and schools now have an exciting opportunity to consider from first principles what secondary school buildings are needed, where they should be and what facilities they should each have ... By targeting a significant proportion of the extra funds on strategic new investments, the additional capital resources could make a much greater impact on educational standards.*

There seems to be no doubt that the commitment, financial and political, is real. In the UK the level of current and projected spending on educational infrastructure has never been greater and the number of properly funded pilot projects for radical new building design are eloquent testimony to the determination to find new ways of creating spaces which will deliver more, more effectively to a much wider target audience.

A new approach to school design

There is therefore powerful and persuasive evidence that this new millennium is very quickly going to produce designs for learning that will finally astonish our Victorian time traveller. The UK government certainly appears to be wholly committed to ensuring that school buildings both enhance and define their core purpose. The UK's Education Secretary wrote in his foreword to Building Schools for the Future (2003):

> *School buildings should inspire learning. They should nurture every pupil and every member of staff. They should be a source of pride and a practical resource for the community.*

There are already plenty of examples of ground breaking and innovative building design. The city technology college and city academies initiatives have produced exciting and quite new approaches to school buildings and it is clear that these pioneering schools are only the beginning of a fundamental revolution in educational thinking.

Case example one

Unity City Academy, East Middlesbrough

Unity City Academy, an 11–16 school with a specialism in ICT, has devised a new language to describe what is a radically new arrangement for learning. There are no traditional subject groupings, the learning is organised conceptually and there is strong encouragement of students to

---

adopt responsibility for their own learning. Teachers incorporate different learning styles (visual, auditory and kinaesthetic) into topics and learning sessions. Students are given the freedom and responsibility to go outside of the normal classroom environment to exercise these different styles, using photography etc.

Case example two

The West London Academy, Ealing

The West London Academy replaced Compton High School and Northolt Primary School with a 4–18 academy specialising in sports and enterprise. Sure Start and adult education provision are also located on the site, as is an LEA maintained special school. The West London Academy has introduced year-basing whereby each year group has its own cluster of classrooms, arranged around a recreation area or 'enterprise zone'. The teachers move between lessons rather than the pupils, giving pupils real ownership of their part of the school.

www.standards.dfes.gov.uk/academies 1997–2004

There are already even more ambitious designs on architects' drawing boards and the UK government's target is to have 53 academies operating by 2007. Equally significantly, this flagship development has attracted well over £100 million from the business and commercial world. This money is only in part philanthropic: major investors in the so called 'real world' are deciding that their involvement in twenty-first century schools can no longer be irregular and largely altruistic. Commercial enterprise must create long and mutually productive partnerships with education if it is to compete on equal terms in an ever more complex and entrepreneurial global market.

Classrooms of the future

In February 2001, the UK government set up a pilot programme, Classrooms of the Future, to encourage educationalists and architects to challenge conventional thinking and create learning environments equipped to meet twenty-first century demands. The brief was that these pilots needed to:

- embrace concepts such as a longer working/learning day and week;
- spread the expertise of the most able teachers more widely;
- integrate developing technologies.

Some of the projects that have now been completed are quite obviously pointing to a future quite unlike anything we have encountered. The new learning schools will use interactive whiteboards, video conferencing, plasma screens and communication links which will enable them to contact communities around the world instantly and comprehensively in ways which will transform learning. E-learning will be firmly established as a tried and tested route for effective curriculum delivery. One of the 12 successful applications for (UK) government funding encapsulates the pioneering spirit at the heart of this initiative.

Case example three

Willow Tree, an 800-pupil primary school in Ealing, London is an excellent example of how proper building design can benefit the learners while helping to reduce running costs. The new school replaces an old sprawling building that was becoming increasingly uneconomic to maintain. Despite the floor area of the new school being about half that of the old, the school is still large but the key is the design that provides an environment conducive to learning. Classrooms are arranged in pairs and in age sequence – nursery, reception, infant and juniors. Each pair of classrooms shares an outside play area, a small cloakroom and a toilet – situated around a central area containing halls, an atrium, shared resources and service areas. With ICT a high priority, the school has been designed with a structured cabling network to provide both voice and data links. This gives direct access to the internet and to large, fixed, interactive whiteboards in each classroom. Teachers can use the internet directly with the whole class – in fact it is possible for all 800 students to use the internet at the same time. This helps to motivate the children as they are able to see their work on the large or small screen. Teamwork is strengthened by teachers e-mailing lesson plans and presentations to all staff members.

Even though we are only at the start of the new millennium, the range and inventiveness being shown in real and proposed designs for school buildings is exciting and innovative. The guiding principles are centred on the need to:

- make it possible for schools to be open far more than they are closed;
- ensure that all those factors that impact on teaching and learning are harnessed for the good of the students.

Negotiating the superhighways

As White (1997) acknowledges there is no question that we now live in the information age:

Whatever we call it, the information revolution, the technology revolution or the digital revolution, the fact remains that now high technology tools are rapidly changing the way people work, the way pupils are taught and the way in which we learn.

Just as significant, the emergence of sophisticated computer hardware and software has taken people on a journey of self-discovery that has made it an imperative that teachers re-examine the way they approach and engage in learning. For instance, the following example is already happening.

Case example four

The cyber teacher

When John Mannion, the only specialist philosophy teacher, left Elliott School in South London, the only solution was for the school to put its trust in the wonders of the video conference screen. Now, the students have lessons on eighteenth century rationalisation taught by a man sitting 50 miles away in Oxford with a laptop computer and a tiny webcam. Students' work is marked via e-mail and Mannion visits the school from time to time in person, a factor helping to keep the process alive.

Quoted in *The Guardian Education Supplement Teach* 2 March 2004 p.9

Crossing new frontiers: the possibilities

Hundreds of millions of people have learnt to use complex software programs, have accessed a bewildering range of e-learning routes, have become totally reliant on e-mail, use video conferencing regularly and work in contexts where access to and use of PCs is second nature. Over the next few years the new frontiers created by nano-technology will be able to produce computers small enough to wear on the body and be powered by the surface electricity of the skin. In the foreseeable future the experience of intelligent computers will make even the astonishing revolution we are currently undergoing in terms of information access look commonplace and ordinary in comparison. The report from the UK's Department for Education and Skills (2002 p.9) clarifies the challenge, as it re-emphasises the growing contribution of ICT to the learning agenda:

Developments in ICT have had, and will continue to have, a profound effect on teaching and learning. Computers are now an essential tool for learning. The number of computers in schools will increase and, in the future, it is likely that all pupils will have their own (wireless) hardware. Electronic whiteboards, scanners and colour printers are also becoming valuable teaching aids. Where practical activities are prohibitively expensive or even dangerous, technology now allows pupils to have 'virtual' practical experience.

The benefits are potentially huge. If twenty-first century schools can utilise for optimum effect the power and range of ICT then they will be much more likely to personalise student learning in ways which will equip the next generation of students to make the most of the information age in which they live. However, there are risks: having access to almost limitless stores of information makes it vitally important that learners develop the skills to be positively selective and constructively critical about what they 'discover'. Equally important, new learning schools must never lose sight of the fact that in a data rich age, a sense of proportion and perspective is crucial.

From school day to learning day

Up until very recently, schools were able to exist quite successfully as self-proclaimed learning centres of the industrial age. They were isolationist and elitist and accepted as such by a society that saw education as taking place within tightly predetermined parameters and learning as being more than anything else received wisdom. Over the last 25 years the pressures on schools to change have been ever increasing. Key factors creating these pressures are:

- increasing levels of public accountability have put schools' measurable performance much more in the social and economic spotlight;
- the opportunities to access formal learning have opened up educational opportunities to a much wider audience. The concept of life-long learning – pioneered by distance learning innovations such as the UK's Open University – is accepted as being valid and worthwhile;
- the emergence of a much more complex knowledge economy has demanded a much better educated workforce;
- self-managing and self-governing schools have become much more aware of the wider market in which they have the potential to operate;
- new technologies have promoted and made accessible the concept of the 24-hour school.

As a consequence, schools have more and more become the hubs of community based learning. These developments have already had, and will continue to have, far reaching implications for the way schools operate in the future as learning organisations. OECD (2001 p.15) suggests:

Teachers in these schools will continue to nurture students but they should not be the only facilitators of student learning. There should be greater reliance placed on community resources to provide teaching and learning experiences for students. The teaching profession needs to broaden its base to admit others to play ancillary but important roles. There are very rich resources for learning in communities – other professionals, artists, gardeners, business owners and so forth – all of whom have the potential to help prepare young people for the future. Schools in the future must be structured in such a way as to facilitate this broad community participation. It is not an exaggeration to refer to 'a new social partnership' for school and their communities.

Teachers: the only resource?

The reference to other rich learning resources in the community is both a vitally important and far reaching observation. For as long as schools have existed the essential truth proclaimed by all those involved in education was that a school's most important resource was its teaching staff; in other words the only people with the expertise and indeed the right to engage in the demanding and complex task of teaching and learning were fully qualified teachers. The extent to which that view has prevailed, not only in staff rooms but also in the mind of most of the public, was tellingly illustrated in the uproar and indignation in the UK at proposals put forward in a Department for Education and Skills' discussion paper (DfES, 2003) to have support staff carry out some of the roles traditionally regarded as the sole province of 'proper teachers'. Professor Ted Wragg, by no means a lone voice, made his feelings crystal clear:

This has clearly been written by somebody who has never been near a classroom. These are dangerous lunatics who should be rooted out and put somewhere safe. This is taking teaching back to the nineteenth century, to Victorian times when anyone was allowed to teach.

However, in considering how new learning schools will be resourced, the following points need to be borne in mind:

- the emergence of a whole new generation of ambitious and talented professionals with the drive and determination to pursue formal routes to teaching and learning qualifications has opened up exciting new models for curriculum delivery;
- as the demand for life-long learning grows and more and more people want to pursue formal training, so the pressures on schools to offer extended educational opportunities increase;
- the new technologies mean that schools will need to become learning centres – accessible far more often and widely by people pursuing ever more sophisticated and specific agendas.

The extended school

Delivering the twenty-first century curriculum through the intelligent use of new technologies, interior and exterior design and much more flexible deployment of teaching and associate staff will render obsolete much of what was considered sound and effective practice as little as ten years ago. The rapid development in the UK of city learning centres points to a very different educational future.

Case example five

Forest Gate City Learning Centre, Newham, London

The specialist ICT facility is used by other schools and adults during the day and evening. The school can also book space. There are three learning areas and a seminar room, with a total of 60 computers. Each space has an electronic whiteboard and the seminar room has video-conferencing and refreshment facilities. The environment and furniture are of good quality. The centre is accessible from the school's main reception area, minimising disruption to the school and reducing security complications. Those attending courses are issued with identification cards which also act as swipe cards.

(Quoted in DfES, 2003 p.24)

If new learning schools are going to have more effective and developed systems to deliver teaching and learning to a much wider target audience, then they should:

- be more accessible more often;
- establish mutually productive partnerships with as many relevant stake-holders as possible.

Schools are already becoming increasingly sophisticated and expensive and national authorities cannot afford to duplicate them. It makes evident sense therefore to group together on one site facilities that are used for adult education, community services, and formal and informal training. This in turn opens up real opportunities for teachers to rethink their roles and take on a range of tasks with learners of all ages. There is really no need for their expertise to be confined to the traditional school day or for assuming that they are only qualified to teach school children.

- there is no reason why teachers should not start their working day at lunchtime and then become adult tutors in the evening;
- if schools are developing rapidly as training centres then teachers and associate staff can deliver training to teachers, trainee teachers, teaching assistants, adults from the commercial/industrial world etc.

In this way learning is going beyond formal education, becoming a lifelong process, helping people to maximise their potential throughout their working and family lives.

Making the change

Creating the positive learning environment

A key theme running through this book is the fact that the challenges facing schools over the next 20 years and beyond are quite unlike anything that has faced schools and school leaders over the previous 200. Schools have always mirrored the world in which they exist; what new learning schools must do is react to and capitalise on entirely new learning opportunities, not least those created by new information technologies. School buildings already exist which reflect twenty-first century teaching and learning needs. However, the vast majority of schools currently in operation have been designed to deliver what is now an outmoded, heavily teacher directed curriculum. A major task facing educationalists, architects and government funding streams is to:

- find a way to modernise these buildings;
- create environments which will allow much greater innovation and flexibility;
- break away from the established so-called truths about what you have to have in a school – like walls, corridors, staffrooms, halls, playgrounds, canteens etc – and really ask the crucial questions about what is essential for effective teaching and learning in twenty-first century schools.

In some cases this may involve something as simple as redesigning interior spaces. There are numerous questions that can immediately challenge conventional thinking, for example:

- If there is wisdom in the concept of the specialist teacher delivering the lead lesson which is then developed by a combination of ICT and associate staff then should we be thinking much more in terms of lecture theatres for say 100 students and larger spaces for flexible teaching and learning?
- How much of conventional experiment-based teaching can be better delivered through computer simulation?
- What part will the fixed computer suite play in the design of new learning schools? Is it more sensible to think in terms of movable laptops that allow every teaching space to become a computer suite – and vice versa? The example quoted shows how current such planning is:

Imagine ICT in every classroom, all over the school. Students going online at their desks instead of having to go somewhere else. E-learning anywhere and everywhere. Collaborating with teachers and fellow students. Sharing work, accessing information, presenting ideas. Imagine what you could do with the ICT room now that you no longer need it. Getting rid of cables, too. This is the power of the wireless network. Accessible, secure, always ready to teach. So if pupils want to study ancient Greece in the canteen, for example, they can.

(Advert placed in the *TES* by a major network provider, 30 April 2004)

- If design technology in the twenty-first century has common themes key to all the so-called discrete disciplines of food, resistant materials, electronics, art, textiles etc, shouldn't we be creating teaching environments which blur the edges and emphasise the features and characteristics common to them all?
- If the evidence suggests that only 30 per cent of the science curriculum requires science laboratories why do we automatically assume that every science teacher always has to teach in one? Building fewer laboratories could compel teachers into rethinking their strategies and approaches to teaching and learning!
- In what ways can we use all available space to optimum effect in order to create an environment that reflects teaching and learning implicitly as well as explicitly? Is it not possible that imaginative use of the school grounds, including linking them to surrounding parks and playing fields for example, can immediately provide stimulating landscaped environments for outdoor learning?
- How can visual display internalise learning? How can we create spaces that students can walk into and unconsciously carry on learning? Do we manage to capitalise sufficiently on implicit learning by, for example, stating in bold large letters around the campus why learning is important and what makes our own particular organisation special?
- How publicly and dynamically do we celebrate the quality and uniqueness of what we do? Professional displays and photographs can make an incredibly powerful impact! The main entrance can speak volumes – good or bad – about the rest of the school. How big and confident is the welcome board/screen for example?
- One school decided to fill a huge empty space larger than a tennis court, with large brilliantly lit photographs of every single student. This spoke more eloquently than any mission statement about the fact that this particular school was there to serve its students.
- How can we make social activities become an integral part of the learning process? For example, The UK's Department for Education and Skills' consultation paper Schools for the Future illustrates how changing the context and the approach to eating food can enhance the learning:

An attractive café-style space that is open all day is more appropriate for a modern learning environment, bringing together pupils, community users and staff. It can become the social centre of the school where parents meet their children and mentors talk to pupils. Longer opening hours will allow pupils to work more flexibly, with less rigid break times, easing congestion at lunch time and possibly reducing the area need. A café can also provide an additional area for informal independent working, making better use of available areas.

(DfES, 2003 p.29)

School buildings should develop the capacity to blur the physical boundaries between formal and informal learning: the less they look and appear isolated from the community, the greater the chances are that they will develop as real community learning centres. There is no question that learning schools will play an integral role in supporting life-long learning and recreation and the way they are designed, remodelled or modified should reflect this.

Capitalising on new relationships

Again there is, clearly, enormous potential for enhanced learning opportunities implicit in the current ongoing technological revolution. For this revolution to make the impact it should, new learning schools will need to ensure that:

- technology becomes a creative tool that encourages learners to be actively engaged in learning rather than a means to avoid thinking for themselves;
- information access develops learning skills and increases creativity;
- personalised learning is encouraged and enhanced;
- work/life balances are improved by allowing greater flexibility in working time and place;
- teaching spaces are utilised to allow efficient and effective access to technologies that are as future-proofed as possible;
- information is presented in ways which will enable learners to make connections, see principles and relate them to their own experiences and emerging sense of identity.

School leaders will need to utilise and deploy these powerful influences sensitively and wisely in ways which will enhance rather than get in the way of effective learning.

Emotional intelligence: making best use of human resources

Even if there were no current and projected teacher shortages, it makes absolute sense to think much more imaginatively about how best to utilise the various skills and experiences of all those capable of delivering effective teaching and learning. There is no doubt that in twenty-first century schools there will be a demand for previously unimagined levels of knowledge and skills. For this to be achieved, a capacity to work in teams will be essential in and for every aspect of educational practice. The pace of change will be relentless so that new learning schools will need to realign resources alongside their underpinning aims and objectives far more frequently than they have ever done in the past. For example:

- if schools are going to broaden their base significantly to offer training on a much larger scale than ever before, then they are going to have to make fundamental changes to the way they employ and deploy staff;
- schools can only develop as twenty-first century learning schools if they commit themselves totally to the principle of promoting and delivering 24-hour teaching and learning;
- new learning schools will also need to take on and capitalise on the potential

strengths and advantages presented by the new technologies. There is no reason why an average size secondary school of say 1,000 students could not in ten years' time be accessed by five times that number of people through distance learning routes.

There is absolutely no way teachers will be able to do this on their own. As a range of professionals from different backgrounds with different skills and a clear set of agendas come into schools to work alongside teachers and learners, so the role and culture of schools will change forever.

References

Beare, H. (2001) *Creating the Future School*. London: RoutledgeFalmer.

DfES (2002) Building Schools for the Future: Designs for Learning Communities, *Building Bulletin 95*. DfES 4.

DfES (2003) Workforce Reform: Blue Skies. Discussion paper. DfES.

Hargreaves, D. (1997) 'A road to the learning society', *School Leadership and Management* 17 (3) p.9–21.

OECD (1995) *Redefining the Place to Learn*. Paris: Organisation for Economic and Cultural Development.

White, J. (1997) *Schools for the Twenty-first Century*, London: Lennard Publishing.

Wragg, E. (2003) 'Workforce Reform Blue Skies', *Times Educational Supplement*, 5 December.

Chapter 7

How We Learn in the 'Classroom'

Preview

This chapter considers the following questions:

- How can we make the most of our immense brain power?
- How can we consistently make classrooms synonymous with learning?
- How is emotional intelligence more important than IQ for learning?
- How can schools develop 'learning to learn' programmes that work?
- How can we motivate young people to engage with learning and become independent learners for life?

> *Learning brings more happiness than having sex, playing or watching sport or doing the national lottery.*
>
> Gallup (1997)

The learning brain

Recent interest in the brain's plasticity challenges notions of fixed intelligence and seems to suggest that if schools and teachers get it right *anyone* can learn anything. On the surface this creates a daunting prospect of a string of new initiatives which may involve the usual endless bureaucratic mound of paperwork and assessment sheets. *However, this particular culture change is not so simple.* If we want to become a truly learning school then we have to have a clear vision of the future and the underlying principles of what sort of school will best prepare its students to be successful citizens in the twenty-first century (as discussed in earlier chapters of this book).

Through the use of magnetic resonance imaging (MRI), neurologists investigating brain activity now know much more about how learning happens in the brain. This work has lent weight to theories of learning which educationalists worldwide have ignored for many years. These include theories of accelerated learning that build on the way the two hemispheres of the brain complement each other; Gardner's (1984) ideas regarding multiple intelligence; Kolb's (1984) cycle of experiential learning that requires a shift 'towards teaching *how* to do something'; Goleman's (1996) seminal work on the impact of emotional intelligence on learning and an increasing awareness of the power of neuro-linguistic programming (NLP) as a tool to facilitate learning. All of these have profound implications for the development of 'learning' in our schools. This chapter examines the implications for the classroom and Chapter 8 links the theory to learning outside the classroom.

It is important to consider some interesting facts about the brain that have come to light in recent research and could change some assumptions about the nature of intelligence.

Important information to consider about the brain

- humans have 100 billion brain cells which learn by making connections;
- every individual brain is different and immensely powerful – enough neurons to store 1,000 CD-ROMS, each one containing the Encarta encyclopaedia;
- we all only use a tiny part (1–5 per cent) of our brain's true capacity;
- all brains thrive in a multi-sensory environment; without stimulation the brain literally shrinks – use it or lose it;
- the human brain needs water and oxygen for thinking.;
- we all learn in very different ways and tapping into those individual learning experiences is essential for students to reach their potential;
- intelligence is not fixed at birth but develops through experience and learning;
- the brain is plastic – which means it changes and grows as we learn.

If we accept any of the above as truths, we need to re-examine the theories of how we learn to lead us to new practice in the classroom and reshape the curriculum to maximise the untapped potential of the human brain. The debate about whether we can nurture an expanding intelligence has been supported by recent research using MRI scans looking at the way specific brain activity develops our brains. London taxi drivers doing the 'knowledge' have clearly defined brain growth around the visual/spatial areas and violinists expand that little part of their brains that focuses on finger movement. These are examples of how specific learning can physically change the brain. This suggests that our brains are constantly changing as we build up connections and embed learning. The capacity we build through learning new skills or information is self-perpetuating – in other words the more you learn the better you are at learning.

Brain plasticity is where, according to Greenfield (2000 p.13) 'physical changes can be seen in the degree and extent of connections between neurons in certain brain regions.' She argues that the 'mind' is being constantly updated 'as the brain becomes more sophisticated … it uses increasingly the results of individual experience, of learning.' Thus the environment and opportunities for learning that are provided have a huge responsibility in developing young minds – whatever brain they are born with.

Figure 7.1 *The triune brain.*

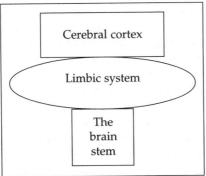

It is the belief that everyone can be an excellent learner that has led to the interest in the work on accelerated learning pioneered by Rose (Rose and Nicholl 1997) and Smith (1998) in the UK. Various publications have explored strategies for 'accelerating' achievement and improving motivation based on research into 'brain friendly' learning.

Smith offers MacLean's 'The Triune Brain' model as worthy of consideration in *Accelerated Learning in Practice,* 1998. MacLean's three-part brain (1990) can be summarised as follows. (See Figure 7.1)

The brain stem or 'reptilian brain' is responsible for survival behaviours and motor functions. The limbic system filters sensory data and emotional responses linked to memory and the neo-cortex deals with higher order thinking. For teachers and schools we can derive the following important notes.

The brain stem or reptilian brain

Responsible for:

- fight or flight and flocking behaviours;
- monitoring motor functions;
- mating rituals;
- territoriality;
- hierarchies;
- rote behaviours.

The reptilian brain state can be bad for learning. When students feel stressed or threatened, defence mechanisms kick in and learning cannot take place. Confrontations that threaten self-esteem will create shutdown. Survival instincts assume priority over logical and creative thinking.

> *The absence of threat is utterly essential to effective instruction. Under threat the cerebrum downshifts … it simply ceases to operate.*
>
> (Hart, 1983 p.3)

This suggests that classroom teachers need to establish positive, productive ritual behaviour such as positive greetings, music on entry to classroom, gestures of praise, affirmations of self-esteem as well as the established behaviour routines such as seating plans, registers, hands up etc. These regular routines are an important part of creating the appropriate state of mind for learning. By creating a 'nest' as a learning environment, where students feel a sense of belonging, the teacher can create a safe comfort zone where students feel receptive to learning. The best classrooms have a clear identity, comfortable chairs, interesting displays and posters with motivational slogans.

Teachers can use the natural tendency of the reptilian brain to seek out group identity by using hierarchies and peer group pressure to motivate by making learning cool for the 'top dogs'. Special awards for contribution to discussion or leadership can be given to the popular and socially accepted students creating a ethos of approval for recognised achievement.

The most important implication for a teacher in the classroom is to avoid confrontations that could create a shift down into reptilian brain state. If a child feels threatened through a teacher shouting or being sarcastic, it is likely that the response will be to 'fight' – argue with the teacher, or shut down the brain's capacity for learning. Any teacher would be wise to avoid confrontation in the classroom in favour of a cooling off period followed by a discussion about issues once the 'thinking brain' has re-engaged. This is important for teacher and student as no teacher can effectively handle such a situation whilst he himself is in reptilian brain state!

The limbic system

The limbic system filters sensory data and emotional responses linked to memory. It also:

- runs emotions via the amygdala;
- governs sexuality;
- is the hub of long-term memory via the hippocampus;
- filters information in and out;
- governs concepts of value and truth;
- validates knowledge and understanding.

Emotions are fundamentally important in learning. We cannot underestimate the vital importance of the limbic system if we are to motivate learners. Its role in learning, emotions and memory has been further researched by Goleman (1996) and Greenfield (2000), amongst many others, and it is now widely accepted to be the gatekeeper of all learning, directing attention to what matters and making essential connections.

'When emotions are engaged, the brain is activated' Jensen's (1995 p.4) extensive research concluded. The chemicals produced when emotions are aroused are 'memory fixatives' as confirmed by Dr James McGaugh, psychobiologist at UC Irvine (in Jensen, 1995) whose research on hormones and emotions led him to conclude that they 'can and do enhance retention.'

How do we engage the emotions for learning? There is some evidence through MRI scanning that our emotional brains respond positively to multisensory experiences such as music, colour, and novelty and enthusiasm. Combine this with a nurturing atmosphere of positive emotions between teacher and students and you have a picture of an excellent learning environment. We also need to accept that high levels of teacher control and 'chalk and talk' without activity and interesting visual aids will not stimulate the emotional brain.

The positive learning environment can be established immediately by a simple smile and greeting students by name as they enter a classroom – an immediate emotional connection. The emotional brain should be engaged from the very beginning of a lesson by making a connection, establishing why the lesson to be learnt is relevant and useful (Smith's WIIFM – what's in it for me?). This is often the lesson objectives and learning outcomes expressed in the teacher's introduction, but the teachers must ensure that these objectives resonate with the students' needs, not just their own.

A lesson taught with enthusiasm and excitement is more likely to engage the emotional brain as the student connects with those emotions. The introduction of a variety of teaching methods including role play, discussion, group work, video, quizzes and interactive whiteboard will keep them engaged. In addition, humour, music and colour are highly stimulating to the limbic system; good teachers make use of this in the classroom. Bringing an element of surprise and novelty to the learning experience makes it memorable, as does clear acknowledgement of success through praise and celebration.

An interactive lesson will be more memorable and engaging for students than one led predominantly by the teacher. This includes interactive approaches to assessment. Self-assessment and peer assessment are considered in Chapter 10. When students are actively involved in all aspects of their learning, the emotional brain is engaged.

The cerebral cortex

Virtually all academic and vocational learning heavily involves the neo-cortex.
(Hart, 1983 p.6)

The cortex deals with higher order thinking, the identification and creation of meaning and long-term planning. It only works when we are able to access it and accessing it requires a shift up into 'the thinking brain' mode. As we have noted, that requires an absence of stress or threat. It is also:

- divided into left and right hemispheres;
- connected via the corpus calossum;
- responsible for cognitive and problem solving functions;

- able to discern relationships and patterns of meaning;
- able to create personal metaphors or models for understanding.

The cerebral-cortex or 'thinking brain' thrives on challenge, feedback and is divided into left and right hemispheres and students often have a hemisphere preference which impacts on their learning. The best learning takes place when both sides of the 'thinking' brain are connected and working together.

Right brain	Left brain
Daydreaming	Logic
Music	Sequence
Intuition	Organisation
Creativity	Language
	Numeracy

The tendency to a hemisphere preference can have implications for teaching style and interventions for inclusions. Research indicates that right brained kinaesthetic learners do find conventional schools very challenging learning environments. Most of the formal, prescribed curriculum suits a left brain dominant ideology with the focus on sequential learning and literacy and numeracy skills underpinning all public examinations. Students need to understand how to develop both sides of the brain through a range of activities that promote whole brain learning. Several UK schools have developed and piloted a learning to learn course with a very positive outcome for students. (See, for example, Beere, 2002). The course develops a language for learning and encourages students to understand the way they learn. It can be delivered as part of the curriculum and/or through a study skills or PSHE programme. As far as the cortex is concerned the aim of any learning to learn course must be to help students learn how to develop their brains to become more able to use both sides fully in whole brain activity that is the most productive for learning. By testing student learning preferences in learning to learn lessons, an action plan can be created to expand the learning repertoires of students.

There are several implications for maximising the potential of the neo-cortex. The cortex thrives on challenge and immediate feedback. In the classroom every teacher needs to create challenge in the form of a 'starter' that stimulates higher order thinking at the beginning of the lesson. Feedback on progress should be as immediate as possible with new targets set at each stage of development. This can be done orally; research shows personal coaching models this practice for maximum progress. Teachers can create the synergy of the left and right brain working together by including creative thinking, for example mind maps or oral brain storms.

When teachers become aware of whether students tend to be left or right brain dominant, they can adapt activity to improve motivation and achievement. For example right brainers could doodle as they are listening or tackle questions in a different order. Often right brained students will have problems with organisational skills and may need support to develop those skills through secondary school. Left brainers, however, could be encouraged to mind map or hypothesise about outcomes before thinking logically.

What is intelligence?

Gardner's theory of multiple intelligence has been the focus of much attention in the UK and USA in recent years. In this section we will look at how this theory can help us engage students in learning and how it could impact on the new learning school.

Sternberg says (quoted in Jensen, 1995):

> *Intelligence boils down to your ability to know your own strengths and weaknesses and to capitalise on the strengths while compensating for the weaknesses.*

He stresses that when we think of intelligence we are really talking about our ability to react intuitively, creatively and constructively to a wide range of experiences. This suggests that a prescribed curriculum does not help students to become more intelligent as it is too knowledge based, without enough encouragement for the right brained thinking activity essential for 'smart' and successful learners.

Mi – the theory of multiple intelligence

Gardner concluded that there are over 200 ways to be smart – some of which depend very much on the culture of the individual. A London stockbroker and an Inuit fisherman can be considered highly intelligent in their own context, even though each would find it difficult to survive in each other's environment. Gardner later grouped the human intelligences into seven categories:

1. **Mathematical/logical – number smart.** *The ability to solve problems, solve maths problems, fix, repair, understand order, do logic puzzles.*
2. **Visual/spatial – picture smart.** *One's relationship to objects and others, reading maps, learning from pictures, maps, diagrams, graphs etc*
3. **Bodily/kinaesthetic – body smart.** *Sports, acting, practical subjects and learning from feeling and doing.*
4. **Musical/rhythmic – music smart.** *Clapping, drumming, composing music, dancing, keeping rhythm, making music.*
5. **Verbal/linguistic – word smart.** *Use of words and language, reading and writing, crosswords, speaking and arguing, explaining, debating.*
6. **Interpersonal – people smart.** *Social skills, cultural bonding, rapport building, empathy, relationships, teamwork and team leading.*

7. **Intrapersonal – self smart.** *Self-awareness, reflection and evaluation, goal setting, diary writing, motivation, deferred gratification, resilience.*

Recently, naturalist and spiritual have been added to this list, with more areas of intelligence still to be identified, according to Gardner.

The usefulness for the learning school of the concept of many ways to be clever is twofold.

(a) Conventional schools do not always value in the curriculum all the different ways to be clever. The focus in schools is very much on 'word smart' and 'number smart' and people who have strengths in these areas are deemed high achievers. Even subjects such as PE which are primarily about 'body smart' skills are assessed using language and number.

(b) Many intelligent learners have been labelled as below average because their assessment did not allow demonstration of their range of abilities. How many young people have left school as failures without the required grades but gone on to become highly skilled mechanics, engineers, plumbers or even entrepreneurs or pop stars?

Helping students understand what their strengths are and how to improve on the weaker aspects of their Mi learning profiles can provide a boost to self-esteem and a range of strategies for improving learning and overcoming motivation barriers. If a student's strength is music smart, he or she can use this to learn maths, if the strength is body smart, kinaesthetic methods can be used to help with spelling and grammar.

Case example one

A large comprehensive school in Northamptonshire

Students in Year 7 test their Mi using a self-assessment questionnaire. They plot the results on a target pie chart and plan how to boost each of their strengths and weaknesses using this knowledge. The results are shared with parents through homework diaries and a workshop where parents are advised how to use the intelligences to help with homework. Each year the Mi profile is updated and students can see how they have grown their preferences and abilities. During exam times, revision programmes are planned that include suggestion of ways to use the Mi model for revision. All departments plan lessons to include use of all seven intelligences throughout the schemes of work and planning over each module. The curriculum is planned to facilitate choice and variety in types of learning and courses that offer a truly Mi approach e.g. media studies, business studies, and leisure and tourism.

Schools need to understand the notion of multiple intelligence and students and teachers need to be aware of their 'smarts' without further labelling creating more barriers. It is clear that the brain grows and changes during the course of a lifetime and especially during childhood. Knowing a child's Mi profile is only a snapshot at that point in his/her development. *The concept of a 'learning school' necessitates a drive towards flexible learning where a student attempts to develop flexibility in learning and growing their potential intelligence across the widest spectrum of skills.* This is why the information derived from self-assessment and Mi testing must be owned by the student and parents and be used as a developmental intervention – not a diagnostic tool for streaming or selection processes.

Lesson planning in all subjects in the 'learning school' could to include all the ways of learning within the scheme of work. This will allow all students to access their strengths and engage in learning. Assessment needs to facilitate different ways to demonstrate learning (see Chapter 10) and schools need to have a full programme of extra curricular activity to develop alternative ways to be smart (see Chapter 8).

Multisensory learning

The nature of all experience is constructed through our five senses. All perceptions are channelled through touch, taste, sight, sound and smell. A baby puts everything to its mouth to learn, a dog will use its acute sense of smell to inform its learning. Humans, as they mature, rely on three of the senses for making sense of the world.

- **Visual**: learning through seeing pictures, videos, displays, books, pictures, maps, mind maps, slide shows and presentations.
- **Auditory**: learning by listening to teachers, each other, tapes and music.
- **Kinaesthetic**: learning through practical work involving activities to reinforce learning, roleplay, drama, brain gym, movement and mime.

This theory originates from the study of neuro-linguistic programming. It was Bandler and Grinder (1979) who first suggested that the way we structure experience involves our five senses, but it is the visual, auditory and kinaesthetic (VAK) that are used by adults in the process of learning. They suggest that there is also the internal VAK. This is the way the brain uses the senses to process information internally, for example, visual images we see inside our heads to help us remember and rehearse future activities. This is an essential part of the way we develop learning as we review what we have experienced – but how do we help students to do this?

Using our internal sensory preferences

When we think, we use VAK to construct or create our memories or our future experiences. We see pictures in our heads that have certain qualities such as colour or movement. We also hear sounds that go with the pictures and get feelings about the events we are envisaging. In this way, we rehearse and review life. It is an essential part of the learning experience and it can help or hinder our progress. When children are learning they are accessing their internal sensory preferences and using techniques such as visualisation. However, some children find it very hard to use these effectively and this often causes barriers to learning. If your visual imaging is weak you will find abstract concepts hard to picture. This is where visualisation exercises can help learning. It is taking the brain's natural activity and nurturing the resources for learning we all have.

In the same way, we all have a continuous internal dialogue that we can use for motivation. When we access our internal dialogue and listen to those conversations inside our heads, we can start to understand how to use them for creating positive learning states. It is rather like cognitive therapy or sports psychology – creating visual, verbal and kinaesthetic experiences of excellent performance or experience that then create self-fulfilling prophecies.

Case example two

A group of Year 11 students in a Learning to Learn lesson spend some time thinking about how they visualise events. They work in pairs to describe to each other how this process works for them and attempt to coach each other in ways to manipulate their thinking. For example, can you turn up the colour and make the sound louder in your memory? In this way they begin to understand how to take control of their thinking and rehearse for exams in a positive way that delivers successful outcomes. They also work on negative internal dialogue that creates self-limiting beliefs, for example 'I'm hopeless at maths' or 'I'm never going to pass'. The session teaches them how to reframe those dialogues and create a bank of positive statements to use when needed.

VAK is about more than the way you prefer to learn – it's also about how we structure experience. Research has suggested through many studies that when learners are taught in their own particular style their motivation, behaviour and achievement improves. In short, they are able to grow their brain and enjoy it! Introducing a topic in the style of the learner, then maximising understanding by using a variety of other inputs to deepen learning, is the optimum method.

Case example three

A group of reluctant learners in Key Stage 4 (15 years-old) had struggled to learn French over a period of two years. The usual techniques of teacher delivery, text books, flashcards and written and spoken activities had not

---

succeeded in engaging the boy-dominated group. They were reluctant to take part orally and some were disruptive. An interactive whiteboard was made available with a range of interactive programmes. Some weeks later, this group were seen completely engaged in a kinaesthetic learning experience, involving an interactive whiteboard and group quiz format. Students were working in competitive groups articulating French and striving to be involved in sharing answers. When tested, their learning was evident through engaging the appropriate senses, making the experience emotional and using their strong interpersonal and physical intelligences.

Emotional intelligence

Goleman (1996 p.xii) asks 'What can we change that will help our children fare better in life?' He concludes that 'there is growing evidence that fundamental ethical stances in life stem from underlying emotional capacities.'

The debate about how we can develop intelligence and help children become motivated independent learners really balances on our readiness to accept a truth long acknowledged by employers and the business community. Emotional intelligence (EQ) is a more important predictor of success than IQ.

There are many baseline tests used in the UK (eg 11+, CATS, MIDYIS and YELLIS) all of which claim to measure intelligence so that we can later see if our students are fulfilling their potential. But they are all based on the traditional notions of IQ linked to linguistic/numeric intelligence that date back to Alfred Binet in 1905, when he was commissioned to identify children who may be in need of special help due to inadequate intellect. This may explain why this data is just part of the picture of our students' potential. Since Binet there have been many other theories of intelligence, most recently the multiple intelligence model (see above), which suggests a variety of ways to be clever, including acknowledging that David Beckham is extremely intelligent on the football field and that Michael Jackson is a musical genius.

In the learning school all the learning styles across the curriculum could be addressed and every student made aware of their Mi profile, and all lessons VAKed. Yet some students will still lack motivation and not achieve their potential because they lack the crucial emotional intelligence that is the real key to successful learning.

What is emotional intelligence? The questions below illustrate some crucial questions about the way we all handle ourselves and our emotions on a daily basis.

- What do you do when you don't know what to do?
- What do you do when you feel unhappy?
- How do you react when someone criticises you?
- How do you feel when you fail?

- How do you make yourself stick to your promises?
- What makes you get up in the morning?
- How do you feel when someone else is successful?
- Do you treat others the way you like to be treated?

It is this form of intelligence that creates the ability to pass or fail – self-awareness, optimism, goal setting, empathy, mood control, deferred gratification, persistence, resilience. The more this can be modelled for our students and our own children, the more successful they will be. We can also teach it and test it explicitly in learning to learn lessons.

Emotional intelligence is the inter- and intra-personal intelligence Howard Gardner identified; however, these are not strongly represented in the current curricula of a number of countries.

A learning school should be an emotionally intelligent institution with the values of EQ – self-awareness, reflective practice, empathy and optimism permeating the ethos and learning environment. All of these are enhanced by a policy of formative assessment (see Chapter 10).

Making the change

The positive learning environment

- Encourage staff to use music in the classroom in all subjects to anchor emotions, for example excitement, relaxation or curiosity. It can also be used to create a calm atmosphere during practical lessons. Avoid allowing students to choose their favourite music as this would then dominate their thinking and create a barrier to learning.
- Check that classrooms are fit for learning. Desks and chairs need to be flexible for group work and comfortable. The temperature should be right for learning – not too hot, not too cold. Displays should enhance peripheral learning and serve as a reference for exemplar work or levels of achievement. Key words and formulas in bright colours are very productive. Motivational posters created by the students can create a positive reinforcement of EQ.
- Can you arrange for the students to be able to drink water in lessons? This will enhance the learning environment. Healthy meals help too!
- Experiment by switching off bells – many schools have done so and found that it works!

Relationships

- Encourage staff to make emotional contact outside the classroom through knowing their students' interests and hobbies, what they are good at and what their problems are. This can make a big difference to building rapport in the classroom.

- Develop a normal routine of staff greeting students by name at the start of each lesson – and with a smile too.
- Develop a procedure of showing students 'what's in it for them' at the start of lessons. Add enthusiasm via 'what's in it for me' also.

Emotional intelligence

- Have you thought of creating a 'learning to learn' course for students that helps them understand the way they learn through creating a learning profile?
- Encourage staff to change student groupings regularly; this will encourage students to push themselves out of their comfort zones.
- Instill in staff the need to take an optimistic approach to student achievement and a belief that intelligence is teachable.

Teaching and learning styles

- Engage staff in knowing their own teaching and learning styles, enabling them to reflect on how it relates to their own classroom practice.
- Support staff in planning their lessons using visual, auditory and kinaesthetic approaches and in utilising access to all the multiple intelligences.
- Develop ways to make students aware of their own learning profile and how to use it in lessons.
- Encourage staff to use brain gym exercises to break up lessons for kinaesthetic learners. Twenty-minute chunks of learning can be broken up by a simple stretch and breathing session.
- Support staff in developing more interactive lessons – for example through student presentations, peer/self-assessment and setting their own tests/ quizzes.
- Encourage teachers to allow students to take down their notes in ways that suit their style. This could include colour, the use of drawings or diagrams or even taping notes for future reference.
- Consider installing interactive electronic whiteboards in classrooms – they can be an excellent prompt for interactive learning.

References

Bandler, R. and Grinder, M. (1979) *Frogs into Princes*. New York: Real People Press.
Beere, J. (2002) *The Key Stage 3 Learning Kit*. Sussex: Connect.
Gardner, H. (1984) *Frames of Mind: The Theory of Multiple Intelligence*. London: Fontana.
Goleman, D. (1996) *Emotional Intelligence: Why It Can Matter More than IQ*. London: Bloomsbury.
Greenfield, S. (2000) *The Private Life of the Brain*. London: Penguin.
Hart, L. (1983) *Human Brain and Human Learning*. White Plains, New York: Longman.
Jensen, E. (1995) *The Learning Brain*. San Diego: Turning Point.
Kolb, D. (1984) *Experiential Learning*. London: Prentice Hall.

MacLean, P. (1990) *The Triune Brain in Evolution*. New York: Plenum.

Rose, C. (2000) *Master it Faster*. London: The Industrial Society.

Rose, C. and Nicholl, M. (1997) *Accelerated Learning for the Twenty-first Century*. New York: Delacorte Press.

Smith, A. (1998) *Accelerated Learning Practice*. Stafford: Network Educational Press.

Chapter 8

Creating the Contexts for Effective Student Learning

Preview

This chapter considers the following questions:

- How can we construct a curriculum that encourages learning to flourish?
- How can we use learning outside the curriculum to enhance the positive learning ethos?
- How can we have a flexible approach to the curriculum that allows for 'personalised' learning?
- How can we create a curriculum which will produce students with the skills, knowledge and experience that the twenty-first century workplace demands?
- How can we make the curriculum flexible enough to meet the needs of learners of various ages and stages of development?

> The curriculum is:
> *Music for the soul, gymnastics for the body.*
>
> Plato

Creating a curriculum structure which liberates learning

Employers of the twenty-first century are showing more dissatisfaction with how schools are preparing young people for the demands of the workplace than ever before. Some of the criticisms include lack of basic literacy and numeracy skills as well as an inability to be creative, flexible and resilient. The latter qualities could be resolved by attention to teaching emotional intelligence as outlined in the previous chapter but the needs of employers will require a more innovative approach to curriculum management than the current prescriptive approaches recommended by previous government agendas. Consideration is being given in UK to a recommendation for a Baccalaureate or diploma approach to education for 14–19 year-olds.

This approach is already used in the International Baccalaureate (IB), with its broad range of compulsory elements including maths, science, languages and

English. Whatever the final form of the prescribed curriculum, there are elements of this award that offer a signpost for the development of curriculum in the twenty-first century learning school. The Community Service and extra curricular elements offer recognition for achievement beyond the classroom and the extended independent study offers an opportunity to pursue personal interests. These features of the IB resonate with the suggested structure for a learning school with a focus on *how* we learn not *what* we learn and a supporting framework of extra-curricular enrichment activity available for students. The approach also raises the status of vocational courses since all students experience a practical work related course and such courses have equal value in accreditation.

> *The brain (is) a jungle ... the learning environment of the classroom should mirror this by inviting challenge and discovery across different domains.*
> (Sylvester, quoted in MacBeath, 1997)

Traditionally, in British schools, the vocational option has been viewed as the lower status qualification. A recognition that students can be clever in different ways, all valuable and useful, will create the ethos for a true learning school where all types of intelligence are developed, and practical skills are nurtured. This future curriculum development, taken in conjunction with the explosion in global e-learning opportunities and the drive to break free from the constraints of a narrow examinations system, may offer unprecedented opportunities for curriculum reform.

How do other countries organise their curriculum on offer? The Norwegian government's curricular aims for the individual, for example, suggest a broad range of educational aims:

- a person searching for meaning;
- a creative person;
- a working person;
- an enlightened person;
- a co-operating person;
- an environmentally sensitive person.

Clearly the issue of curriculum leadership and reform is a global concern and begins with a search for the purpose of education itself. If our purpose in education and schooling is to fulfil the potential of learners and develop independent learners for life then our current system with its prescriptive and restrictive curriculum is not succeeding. Our present system restricts students to taking examinations at certain ages and certain times of the year. A vision for the future presents a 'multi-age, multi-status, mixed ability, teamwork' approach using alternative forms of assessment for different learners (Jensen, 1995). With students of various ages learning together in a classroom and progressing at various stages according to individual strengths and needs, a picture of truly personalised learning curricula begins to emerge.

The importance of looking at the curriculum as a whole is identified by Middlewood (2001 p.109) as operating at four levels:

1. *The rhetorical curriculum*: what is stated in policies and statements of aims.
2. *The planned curriculum*: found in schemes of work, syllabuses.
3. *The delivered curriculum*: how it is taught in the classrooms or through other media.
4. *The received curriculum*: what is ultimately in the mind and some would say the hearts of the students.

These four levels can only be in harmony when the aims and values of the school drive decision-making to put student learning at the centre. The hierarchy of needs for creating the 'learning school' begins with the fundamental need to create the environment for learning. This environment for learning embraces the 'hidden' curriculum where informal everyday opportunities and events create another layer of learning for students. This includes everything from holding a door open to strangers to computer club or netball practice after school.

Creating a whole school policy for teaching and learning is one effective method of helping to ensure that the curriculum is delivered in a way that is harmonious with a school's aims and objectives to promote innovative and engaging learning. In school improvement studies, Hopkins et al (1994) have shown this type of guidance can be beneficial to student learning. It could be argued that the content is less important than adherence to the principles of effective processes outlined in Chapter 7. If children can learn how to learn, the content of their learning is less important than their ability to reflect and learn from experience through metacognition. (See Figure 8.1)

Figure 8.1 *Contexts for school learning.*

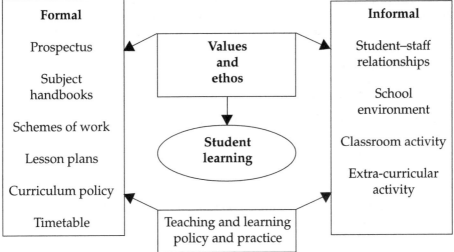

Problems of implementation of curriculum changes, explored by Fullan (1991) have been a consequence of a failure to address the people-related aspects of curriculum change, sometimes exacerbated by inadequate staffing in schools. A focus on teaching and learning as opposed to content of the curriculum is more realistic for twenty-first century schools. So does it matter what we teach? The skills of ICT, communication, creativity, literacy, numeracy and citizenship may provide the twenty-first century learning school with a framework for a new curriculum model. Link these competences with the multiple intelligences model – as described in the previous chapter – and a skills based curriculum emerges.

Can we design such a curriculum within a national framework such as that in the UK? Can we be more flexible and creative yet work within the fundamental principles of brain-friendly learning? These are:

- *choice* – which creates commitment and ownership;
- *connections* – as learning that connects with real life works more effectively;
- *variety and breadth* – growing brainpower means developing all the intelligences.

The National Curriculum for the UK is a document that outlines what needs to be taught. An alternative approach would be a curriculum that focuses not on content, but on skills to be developed.

An alternative approach

The Royal Society for Arts (RSA) has piloted a competency based curriculum for Key Stage Three (12–14 years) which has shown many benefits including raising achievement and a positive impact on transition from primary to secondary phase. The principles of this curriculum model are that students are taught by a smaller number of teachers in a **project based** format that tracks the prescribed subjects within a cross curricular activity. So the model looks at the *skills* that we require students to develop rather than the knowledge that we feel they should gain. Each project aims to develop the competencies below.

The RSA competence framework

This has five competencies expressed in terms of outcome:

Competences for learning

Students would:

- understand how to learn, taking account of their preferred learning styles;
- understand how to manage their own learning throughout their lives;
- learn, systematically, how to think;

- have explored their creative talents and how to use them;
- have learned how to love learning for its own sake;
- have achieved high standards in literacy and numeracy and special understanding;
- have achieved high standards in handling information and communications technology.

Competences for citizenship

Students would:

- have developed an understanding of ethics and values and how personal behaviour should be informed by these including how to contribute to society;
- understand how society, business and government work;
- understand and value cultural and community diversity;
- understand the social implications of technology;
- understand how to manage their lives including financial awareness.

Competences relating to people

Students would:

- know how to relate to others in varying contexts;
- understand how to operate in teams and various team roles;
- understand how to develop and coach others;
- have developed a range of communication techniques;
- have developed competence in managing personal and emotional relationships;
- understand various means of managing conflict.

Competences for managing situations

Students would:

- understand the importance of managing their own time and develop preferred techniques for doing so;
- understand what is meant by managing change and have a variety of techniques for varying situations;
- understand the importance of celebrating success and managing disappointment;
- understand what is meant by being entrepreneurial and initiative-taking and how to develop these capacities;
- understand how to manage risk and uncertainty in a wide range of contexts and learn techniques for managing them.

Competences for managing information

Students would:

- have developed a range of techniques for accessing, evaluating and differentiating information, to analyse, synthesise and apply it;
- understand the importance of reflecting and applying critical judgement.

In practice these competences could be delivered at this stage through project work, at the same time meeting National Curriculum content requirements.
For example:

Project title: The Olympic Games

Content:

- history of the tradition of the Games;
- mapping the places the Games have been held;
- a database of results of different countries;
- a story/diary entry for an athlete;
- a news story for local or regional press;
- a study of the psychological or physiological processes involved in peak performance;
- a practical activity relating to Olympic events;
- an internet research project on a famous athlete;
- a debate in Parliament about the pros and cons of hosting the Games;
- designing and creating posters and pictures by hand and using computer packages.

The list of ideas is endless!

A typical Year 7 student (11 year-old) would spend 50 per cent of the timetable in competence lessons and the rest in core subjects, thus decreasing the numbers of teachers and the compartmentalisation of the curriculum. Clearly this curriculum model owes much to the primary sector and could provide a smooth transition into more in-depth subject study later in the next Key Stage.

A key factor in creating this curriculum is to overcome the traditional secondary school 'dip' in achievement that comes from the students failing to transfer skills from one subject to another as they move stages or schools. Another is to make school fun!

The opportunities for flexibility and choice can be an integral part of the post-14 options in the curriculum. Fast-tracking students and offering a variety of vocational and academic choices up to and including Distance Learning Degree modules will need to be part of the twenty-first century learning school ethos.

Case example one

A flexible course in learning to learn

A secondary school created a new course called Learning to Learn accredited by the Open College Network at Level 1 or 2. Students opted in to it at Year 10 (15 years old) and the scheme included investigating their learning profile before planning a number of learning projects. The learning projects were linked to their learning profile and targets for expanding their multiple intelligences and their emotional intelligence. For example, learning to juggle, reading instructions, watching someone else, practising in planned stages using persistence, mood control – body smart and people smart. The assessment was through evaluation, presentations and demonstrations of skills to the group. Coaching and learning to coach each other was an underlying principle of learning together and became a powerful model for discovering how to learn effectively. Other projects such as learning to use a digital camera, learning to ride a unicycle, learning some tai chai moves, choreographing a dance, learning how to practise holistic medicine were chosen by the students. A large mural was painted by students on one project and a multisensory garden was created by another group. All the students achieved at least Level 1 in the course, with 90 per cent achieving Level 2.

The prescribed National Curriculum in England has tended to promote a transmission approach to learning, with the student assumed to be an 'empty vessel' into which the expert teacher pours knowledge. This regime of passive learners and expert teachers culminates in the late twentieth century trend of 'teaching to the test' to boost league table position, resulting in students not having the skills or the independence to transfer learning to other aspects of life experience. As Claxton (1997) suggests, 'towing them through the tests' disempowers learners and makes teachers work harder than ever. The twenty-first century learning school needs to adopt a much more interactive approach to learning and the curriculum. This will inevitably lead to a blurring between what is taught inside and outside the curriculum.

Other opportunities for student learning – curriculum extra

Handy (1997 p.163) suggests that life skills are vital for the 'portfolio people' of the twenty-first century who will have several careers and need to constantly update skills and manage their career paths. Handy also suggests that, amongst other ideas, 'intuitive, emotional, interpersonal' intelligences or talents need to be addressed in schools. A picture is emerging of the need for a skills-based, independent, self-motivated learner with good communication skills and excellent personal initiative.

Where would we find such qualities being developed through choice and self-direction, reinforcing commitment and teamwork, flexibility and independence? In after school clubs, debating societies, sports teams, drama productions, school magazine or yearbook production teams, choirs or big bands – in fact any activity that is extra to the 'classroom curriculum' offered by the school.

Case example two

A large secondary school offers an extra period 3.30–5.30 pm for enrichment activities every day. The students choose from a huge range of voluntary activities delivered by teachers and support staff. In addition there are master classes run in the holidays offering extension study in certain subject and links with business for extended work experience. The school day begins with a breakfast club at 8.00 am and finishes at 13.50 pm on Friday. Students are encouraged to track their learning programmes across the compulsory and voluntary curriculum and all achievement is acknowledged and valued by special awards from the headteacher.

In developing a curriculum that is appropriate for current and future needs of society and communities, it can be argued that we need to think beyond the confines of a subject based curriculum to include debate on the sort of society we want. This view stresses the need to link school, non-school and lifelong learning, reflecting a holistic view of learning and life. Connecting learning to leading a successful and happy life requires more than prescribing a list of subjects and skills. An emotionally intelligent society is empathetic, reflective, self-aware and continually learning. For schools to create individuals with these qualities, this requires them experiencing success as learners and connecting this success to the value of learning as a lifelong pursuit. Students experience most success in learning in their chosen extra-curricular activities.

Schools need to be able to offer a range of activities every day, during breaks between lesson times and after school. These can be delivered by teachers or support staff depending on the skills and talents available in the school community. The activities could range from chess club to self-defence, aerobics to debating society, cookery club to reflexology. In addition the full range of sports and games should be offered to students regardless of their ability to 'make the team'. The teamwork required for all sports is an essential requirement for developing EQ and leadership skills. Performing arts productions of all types and scales are powerful learning experiences especially if the organisation and production are led by students.

Visits to theatres, museums and areas of natural beauty linked to the curriculum provide the memorable emotional impact that can 'anchor' learning. School residential experiences often provide opportunities for team building, self-development and growth that can have a lasting impact on students' attitude to school life and learning. Where students succeed less well in the classroom, they can earn respect and friends when abseiling down a high cliff or supporting their team to build a raft to cross a river. Residential trips develop essential interpersonal and intrapersonal skills as they require children to work together in novel situations which may challenge their comfort zones.

Ask any student what they can remember about the last three years at school. It will be something funny or unusual or most likely a trip, visit or residential they have been on.

Cross curricular events

Creating events that allow students to break free from the routine of the timetable often establishes a learning breakthrough. Many schools often introduce an industry day or business and enterprise events to introduce senior students to local employers and enable them to take part in a marketing or production exercise. This can be an excellent opportunity for students to 'step out of school uniform and into office dress' for the day (sometimes literally so) and investigate their leadership and teamwork skills in a role play exercise. Specialist Schools in the UK hold community events that relate to their specialism such as international days for language colleges. These provide ideal opportunities to reinforce the ethos of tolerance, empathy and understanding of other cultures as they experience cooking, singing, dancing and communicating through video conferencing with schools across the world. An even more innovative approach is to have thinking skills days or super learning days giving students an opportunity to reinforce work done on learning to learn programmes by clarifying their learning profiles and how to use them.

Case example three

An urban school invited a selection of students from the secondary sector and their partner primary cluster schools and booked a local prestigious venue for a Super Learning day. The morning was spent with a visiting speaker and lots of motivational activities. The afternoon was spent in multi-age groups planning a PowerPoint presentation called 'Creating the school of the future'. Parents were invited in for the presentations and special awards were made for achievement on the day.

After students have sat formal tests at set times of the school year, it is often hard to motivate students via the normal timetable. A week off timetable committing to a sustained learning experience chosen from a selection of projects such as digital photography, a dance production, producing a school yearbook, becoming a football referee, working for a first aid qualification, producing a promotional leaflet for local amenities etc is a constructive way of re-engaging students in learning for its own sake.

115

Another approach to the curriculum for 14 year-olds is to offer target groups of students opportunities to meet their needs in alternative ways. Partnerships between further education colleges, businesses, colleges and schools can offer practical and vocational options either by transporting students to colleges or importing the teachers and resources to set up a car service workshop or hairdressing salon. Another alternative is a community service option for students who would benefit, and get them out into the community working as decorators and gardeners or running bingo sessions for those who need such services. As disaffected students are often identified as being in danger of exclusion, this group can be targeted for intervention approaches that develop emotional intelligence and a sense of responsibility in a group setting.

Opportunities to develop leadership skills through older students leading activities for the younger age groups are not always exploited fully. The learning school for the future needs to be continually looking for ways in which students can act as role models for younger students by running computer clubs, football teams, leading assemblies or sharing their skills in self-defence or video editing. This is a winning strategy for all involved and can be extended in age down to primary schools where students can teach basic French to youngsters or lead art and craft sessions.

Case example four

A drama Advanced Skills Teacher developed a course of thinking skills and EQ that is used as an optional intervention with students identified as challenged by the school demands. They meet as a group on a weekly basis and talk through issues and challenges with teachers sharing advice about how to deal with negative feelings. In this way students at risk of exclusion have remained at school and attained a set of useful qualifications. The AST is then able to share her programme with other schools via outreach work and set up cross-school liaisons for students and teachers. She is now training a team of six youngsters to work with the primary sector using a masks workshop to identify feelings and talk through scenarios.

ICT and learning outside the curriculum

A programme of learning outside the curriculum within the school or organisation can now be integrated with e-learning to create an interactive global learning experience that has massive potential to re-engage learners. From the development of the BBC's GCSE 'Bitesize' interactive revision programmes, to the online courses published through the school's own website, the learning school needs to make full use of the opportunity for extended learning that ICT presents. Ultimately a student who struggles to cope with the school as an institution can access a wide curriculum through a tutorial programme called notschool.net, and this includes full accreditation.

Cyberspace is offering an alternative approach to learning. Interactive websites, video conferencing and the online curriculum mean that students are no longer necessarily tied to school premises for learning opportunities. As the capacity for monitoring and assessing achievement on line increases, the challenge of integrating face to face delivery with independent learning via the internet is one the effective learning school will relish.

Case example five

A 14 year-old boy, academically gifted but suffering from a behaviour dysfunction leading him to threaten and intimidate others, was offered a programme of home based study through not school net as an alternative to permanent exclusion. The school kept him on their official register but handed over assessment, tuition and monitoring to the online learning community and the development of his social needs to his family. Within six months, he had taken and passed examinations, joined a rugby team and the Air Cadets. He is no longer the angry, frustrated bully and social outcast but is becoming a worthwhile citizen who wants to be a lawyer.

November (2001) suggests that the internet and online learning gives us an amazing insight into just how much young people want to learn. A huge amount of self-directed education already takes place outside of school through the web. Students are creating and sharing their own websites, posting stories and articles on line for review from their peers across the other side of the world. Encouragingly, many are in a constant dialogue of reflection about their achievement. For example on www.fanfiction.net children as young as 10 are publishing stories based on models of writing such as the Harry Potter books. These stories are then posted for review with hundreds of hits from other writers across the world and the feedback is used for young authors to rewrite their stories and improve their reviews. All this happens without the extrinsic motivation of exam grades and teacher approval. No learning school for the twenty-first century can afford to ignore the message contained in this evidence. When young people are motivated by their peers to develop their learning and skills, they will be excellent learners. Many hours are spent by young people on the net seeking out information on subjects that matter to them – things they can connect with, whether it be music or chemistry. Chat rooms and message centres are alive with activity 24 hours a day, seven days a week. How can we harness that commitment to communication skills in our schools?

The real revolution in learning is not about adding technology on top of the current structure of school. Instead, the real revolution is about a transformational shift of control from the school system to the learner.

(November, 2001 pp.xv-xvi)

Learning in school outside the curriculum needs to be mapped. As we have noted, some of the most powerful learning experiences at school are derived from the culture and everyday practice of the school. Many of these provide opportunities to promote the ethos of the learning school and engage young people in positive attitudes that will develop resilience and successful strategies for learning for life.

A persistent difficulty in managing the curriculum is the temptation to break off curriculum and treat it separately.

(Lofthouse, 1994 p.7)

This has created the balkanisation of subject departments, defending their right to teach their 'bit' without a sense of the big picture of the school's needs. It is essential that all staff are engaged in the holistic approach to planning learning for the whole child.

In the UK it is a statutory obligation for each student to experience an act of Christian-based collective worship every day. For most schools this causes many problems, many of them related to a venue big enough to house all the students and the mix of Christian and non-Christian students. A compromise is usually reached whereby assemblies for year groups are held with a moral or spiritual theme led by various school leaders. This presents an ideal opportunity for students to become involved in planning and presenting their own assemblies relating to areas of citizenship or spirituality that interest them. Research has shown that when the message is delivered by students' peers it is more memorable and convincing to the audience.

Tutorials, registration and PSHE (personal, social and health education) offer the learning school opportunities to be innovative. A learning family structure for tutor groups would offer students grouped vertically shared experiences and life skills across age barriers. Schools that have used this method of social grouping have found it promotes a sense of responsibility and community, thereby reducing bullying and intimidation. If this is not a possibility, a house system where vertical grouping complements horizontal grouping can offer an inclusive approach to school community activities.

Learning to learn programmes and ICT can be delivered to these mixed age groups, thus eroding the traditional restrictions of age-related learning and expectation. These groups also lend themselves to highly effective 'community of enquiry' approaches to learning. All students benefit from the shared experiences and support. The development of flexible communication skills and rapport with peers of differing ages are a clear advantage to students experiencing this type of tutorial programme.

Case example six

A secondary school in Dudley decided to group students into vertical families for all non-curricular activities. In each form there are four Year 7/8/9/10/11 students, and six sixth form students are also part of the group. Students stay in these groups for most of the Citizenship programme and each year group advises their classmates when important landmarks arrive such as GCSE choices. Circle time is an important part of the tutorial programme which involves students talking freely about concerns around school life.

Peer mentoring and student voice

School life offers many opportunities for learning, and the voice of the student in contributing to decision-making and school development is a crucial part of the school of the twenty-first century. In the UK, student councils have traditionally restricted their discussions to the state of the toilets and designing new uniforms, but a culture of student participation is developing in many schools mirroring that of many other countries in the West. This includes responsibilities for interviewing potential teachers, sitting on the governing body and taking a leadership role across the school in a variety of ways. Developing leadership skills and a sense of responsibility for the culture of the school is an essential part of the 'hidden' curriculum that can be fostered in this way.

The opportunities for learning and developing emotional intelligence via this participation are endless. Peer mentoring involves training and supporting youngsters to provide a coaching and advice service for their peers. This has resulted in benefits for both the recipient and the mentor as each form positive relationships and develop life skills through the experience. This involves students giving up their own free time to help others and although it needs teachers to monitor and support, it is an activity that schools can set up fairly easily.

Case example seven

Twelve year-old students volunteered to 'buddy' a student from Year 7 during registration once a week at an East Midlands school in England. They were given a folder with the types of questions to discuss over a drink and biscuit at lunchtime on the first meeting, then they met regularly at registration for a year. Some relationships didn't work and opt-outs were available, but 75 per cent of the students in both year groups reported that they enjoyed the experience and have made good friendships. 'I liked it when he helped me with my homework' was one comment! Some students arranged their own meetings outside of the designated times and the Year 7 students were keen to act as 'buddies' for the following year's intake.

To summarise, a twenty-first century learning school could move away from the content-driven school diet of every British student in the twentieth century and into a much more skills-based environment where the emphasis is on working with the brain to engage learners in a process of discovery that will create independence and personal growth. That personal growth can be enhanced by opportunities for self-directed learning in an extensive programme of enrichment activities offered within and beyond the school day. All learning can have a relevance that connects it to real life and a range of teaching and learning styles will make this curriculum accessible for all students. A student emerging from this type of school will be very different from the student that employers at the start of the twenty-first century are regularly castigating for lack of basic skills, initiative and emotional intelligence.

A learning school is prepared to evaluate its curriculum provision through a curriculum review process that takes account of the views of teachers, students, parents and external auditors such as school inspectors. A rolling programme of self-review reporting to governors facilitates an open approach to school development which befits an emotionally intelligent institution.

Making the change

The positive learning environment

- Try creating a flexible curriculum that allows students choice and encourages commitment. If students can move through at their own pace, progress could be linked to attainment not age. This opens up the possibility of students of various ages being taught together and progressing when they are ready.
- Identify ICT learning opportunities to support curriculum delivery and provide opportunities for students to use facilities outside of lessons.
- Use a Whole School Review programme where each subject is reviewed using student voice input, lesson observation and sampling of work.
- Offer as many opportunities for 'curriculum extra' activities within and after the normal school day as possible; ensure this achievement is recognised and rewarded at the highest level to encourages commitment and motivation.
- The school calendar should include cross-curricular events such as International Citizenship Day, Industry Day or opportunities for independent learning.

Relationships

- Using a Whole School Review process, ensure curriculum development is staff and student led and owned. In this way, relationships will benefit from sensitivity to each other's needs.
- Try to offer residential experiences early in the school career and as often as possible throughout school life to develop good relationships with staff and good interpersonal skills.

- Create a supportive ethos through peer mentoring across and within year groups.
- Encourage a student voice facility to involve students in decision-making and school improvement initiatives.

Emotional intelligence

- Try to encourage a wide range of additional activities. All 'curriculum extra' develops emotional intelligence because students are choosing to learn and learning across subject boundaries.
- Include a 'learning to learn' programme within the curriculum with an underpinning of EQ elements. Each subject could audit the EQ in each lesson planned and ensure that elements of EQ are at work in as many lessons as possible.
- Ensure well managed classrooms that teach about rights and responsibilities. Try including 'thinking sheets' for students to reflect on how their behaviour could be different next time. The process for punishment should be consistent and clear in its structure so that students can learn to control their behaviour and choose to take decisions that help their learning.

Teaching and learning styles

- Help students and teachers to understand their learning profile to address their learning needs in all subjects. Students will need to understand that they won't find all learning easy and this means they need to work harder at some subjects to achieve progress.
- The whole school curriculum needs to address all the intelligences to allow all students to achieve their potential. Try to ensure that lesson planning takes account of learning styles and offers a variety of approaches.
- Create a differentiated curriculum that includes attention to learning styles. Alternative curriculum approaches may be offered to students who benefit from, say, a more practical approach.

References

Claxton, G. (1997) *Hare Brain, Tortoise Mind*. London: Fourth Estate.

Fullan, M. and Stiegelbauer, S. (1991) *The New Meaning of Educational Change*. New York: Teachers College Press.

Handy, C. (1997) *The Hungry Spirit*. London: Hutchinson.

Hopkins, D., Ainscow, M. and West, M. (1994*) School Improvement in an Era of Change*. London: Cassell.

Jensen, E. (1995) *The Learning Brain*. San Diego: Turning Point.

Lofthouse, M. (1994) 'Managing the Curriculum', in T. Bush and J. West-Burnham (eds) *The Principles of Educational Management*. London: Pitman.

MacBeath, J. (1997) 'Unlock the secrets of the thinking brain', *Times Educational Supplement*, 20 June, p.22.

Middlewood, D. (2001) 'Leadership of the curriculum: setting the vision', in D. Middlewood and N. Burton (eds) *Managing the Curriculum*. London: Paul Chapman.

November, A. (2001) *Empowering Students with Technology*. New York: Pearson.

Chapter 9

Learning and Transition

Preview

This chapter considers the following questions:

- How far do current structures and traditions support effective transition?
- How far can transitional learning be personalised?
- What role will the new technologies play in transition?
- How are we to match individual needs to corporate structures and assessments?

> *Life is seamless, so is learning. Why can't education be so?*
>
> Peter Coleman

Transition requires movement

'Transition' describes the process whereby an individual moves from one set of circumstances to another. There is a built in assumption in this definition that each change of circumstance will carry with it a sense of development or progress. In essence, the educational system that has operated in the UK and elsewhere for the last 200 years has fostered a culture which celebrates the fact that the learning which takes place in one school phase is by and large unique to that phase. In the UK for example there are:

- *learners who are in early years classes or nursery school;*
- *learners who are in reception classes;*
- *learners who are in infant school;*
- *learners who are in junior school;*
- *learners who are in secondary school;*
- *learners who are in FE/HE;*
- *learners who are in adult education.*

In the UK there are even teaching strategies which are linked with particular key stages, i.e. the numeracy and literacy strategies at various Key Stages.

Traditionally in this country, and in many other countries worldwide, the move in educational terms from one set of circumstances to another involves a change of physical surroundings, i.e. a new school. Equally traditionally, there is widespread ignorance on the part of educational practitioners about the style, content and pedagogy of learning phases they are not directly involved in. By linking the idea of transition with physical movement, an immediate casualty is the notion of being able to change circumstances while still in the same physical context. In twenty-first century learning schools such compartmentalisation of learning needs to be challenged. If we take transition as seen as implying moving from one set of circumstances to another, we need to see this in terms of 'learning' not in terms of 'transferring to other schools'.

Many secondary schools at present fall into the habit of assuming the 'big' transition has occurred when students arrive and they then allow their systems to take over. Consider school uniform, for example. It may be reasonable for a school uniform to signify pride in a new base at 11 years old, but most schools only then make adjustments – or concessions as they are usually termed – to rules about uniform when students reach post-compulsory age or sometimes the final year of statutory schooling. In no family would it be considered appropriate to treat a 15 year old the same as an 11 year-old brother or sister. Families show an awareness that children have passed through enormous transitions during that period.

Transition happens in stages

'Transition' also implies 'stages'. There have been many writers, most notably Shakespeare with his seven ages of man, who have attempted to view life as a series of pre-determined phases. Erikson (1977) has suggested that life can be viewed as being in various stages, each of which involves transition (the ages are approximate and constantly shifting in terms of human development):

- *infancy (0–2): trust v mistrust;*
- *early childhood (2–4): autonomy v shame and doubt;*
- *play age (5–7): initiative v guilt;*
- *school age (6–12):industry v inferiority;*
- *adolescence (13–19): identity v role confusion;*
- *young adulthood (20–30): intimacy v isolation;*
- *maturity (30–60): generativity v stagnation;*
- *old age (60+): integrity v despair.*

There is no doubt that seeing transition as being made up of such clear and distinct phases can be helpful, especially in terms of interpreting the emotional context of the learner. Nonetheless, such a viewpoint carries with it the inescapable reality that we all broadly progress at the same rate and behave in the same way. At the centre of the learning philosophy in twenty-first century schools must be the public and confident acknowledgement that each person's transitional journey is made at his/her own speed and that that journey develops in ways unique to the individual concerned.

Impersonal journeys

Although all countries have their own models of when these transfers take place, certain features emerge as common to all:

- the move from one stage to another inevitably involves leaving one familiar place and starting at another wholly new one;
- such a move is as emotionally charged as it is educationally driven – perhaps more so;
- great emphasis is placed on the maintenance (and in some cases the dismantling) of established friendship groups;
- learners almost inevitably – as a consequence of the educational and emotional upheaval of moving from one phase to the next – suffer a performance dip; in the UK this is particularly evident in Year 4 (8 year-olds) Year 5 (9 year-olds) and Year 8 (13 year-olds);
- the learning style of one stage is often significantly different from the established learning practice of the next;
- the communication and knowledge transfer systems between stages are largely under-developed, under-used and mutually undervalued by teachers;
- each end of stage is linked to some form of formal public assessment.

In learning schools, transition should be seen not as a series of chronologically inevitable physiological obstacles to be accepted and somehow overcome, but rather as a learning journey – a journey which is in fact as seamless and naturally sequential as possible and made at a pace which suits the individual. Learning schools will put the learners, not management systems, at the centre of everything they do. Currently, however, education systems do not work like this. Instead:

- all journeys start from the same place at the same time;
- people's speed is dictated by the speed of the majority;
- learning is viewed as happening in pre-determined stages when it is, in fact, a continuous process;
- too much energy is being spent on smoothing the transfer process rather than making sure that student learning is sustained and enhanced;
- too many schools promote the 'fresh start' approach to transition which confuses learners;
- transfer to a new school can often result in a decline in progress which triggers a loss of enjoyment and decreased motivation.

Case example one

Johns Hopkins University in Baltimore, USA, runs gifted and talented programmes for the top 1–2 per cent of the population. One 14 year-old boy was given a mathematics problem to solve unaided. After he had solved it he moved on to the next concept – again unaided. After eight hours he had completed the national programme of study for his peer group designed to last for the whole academic year – all with no teacher input. Imagine the potential here for boredom, disruption and disaffection!

Personal journeys

If we see transition as a journey, then 'personalised learning', the concept being promulgated by the UK School Standards Minister, which demands that every aspect of teaching is designed around a learner's needs, inevitably means that no two journeys will be the same.

Case example two

In 1987, 100 14 year-old students in a large comprehensive school in the north of England spent a week 'discovering' Australia. Two whole days were given over to finding out in detail as much as they could about the Aborigine way of life. They discovered that Aborigines lived life as a journey and that everyone had to make their own journey in line with their individual preferences, strengths and aspirations. The students decided that they would create their own journeys, set their own targets, put aside time to reflect and decide where they were going and when and how they planned to arrive. Particularly significant was the fact that the students set themselves more demanding targets and decided to embark on much more complex and challenging learning pathways than those pre-determined 'journeys' planned by their teachers who were following nationally constructed curriculum directives. Learners will, it would appear, like the Aborigines, make their own journey in their own time and place and at their own speed.

Effective transition will allow learners to move at a pace which is right for them and take pathways which reflect their strengths and aspirations. However, it is difficult to see how such an approach could be managed on a large scale. Leadbeater (2004 p.18) explains:

A universal, personalised learning service would indeed be a revolutionary goal. By giving the learner a growing voice, their aspirations would become central to the way services were organised. At the moment the heart of the system are its institutions that lay down what education is and how it should proceed. Studies of performance management across a wide range of organisational fields show that productivity invariably rises when people have a role in setting, and thus owning, their targets. The same is true for learning.

In the UK at present the government has put in place heavily prescriptive systems that dictate what education is and how it should proceed. Children beginning their education in England at age 4 will be formally tested 137 times by the time they reach 18. They will take nationally formulated tests at 7, 11, 14, 16, 17 and 18 and there are plans to introduce further formal tests at 5. A particular casualty of this system is the 16–19 cohort, the age of transition:

- when minds are beginning to develop and take shape;
- when opinions, learning styles and long-term goals are being fine-tuned;
- when attitudes and aspirations are being set down which will dictate much of what happens to these learners for the rest of their lives;
- where the journey is as important as the destination;
- when exploration and questioning should be the norm;
- when following interesting tangential diversions should be actively encouraged;
- where space needs to be created for learners to challenge, expand and dissect established educational, social and moral truths.

Instead, this time of unique growth is crammed into 18 months of rote learning, didactic teaching and examination overload. This cannot be right now and will not be right for twenty-first century learning schools.

Transition: creating the opportunities

Much of this chapter thus far has concentrated on what prevents and frustrates effective transition. The task for the learning school is to see transition as an exciting opportunity to guide, coach and support learners to develop the skills and the courage to embrace and take up their own personal journeys. We have already made some mention of the UK government's current advocacy of personalised learning. However, creating a system which is fluid enough to achieve such an objective is a huge undertaking. Gibbons (2004 p.30) argues:

It is challenging to provide a personalised experience which still exhibits features of nineteenth century origin. Education today could be said to echo the Fordist principle of standardised mass production. This means that personalised learning is delivered in a culture of public service which traditionally fits the individual to the system, not the other way round.

Fitting the system to the individual is a simple aim to articulate; however, the logistical and structural implications are, of course, huge. In examining this, Leadbeater (2004 p.11) introduces us to the concept of the 'Learning Pathway':

> *In a personalised system, students might be able to choose whatever options or modules appealed to them. The challenge here would be to reduce the risk attached to one choice. In other words, the learning pathways of students would become far more flexible. Learners could make choices right along the pathway rather than simply at the gateway, as happens now.*

Not just at the gateway

Leadbeater's view seems to fit with what would make for effective transition in twenty-first century schools. Although there might well be changes of schooling along the way, what Leadbeater is suggesting here is a system which would allow a freedom of choice and diversity of routes unlike anything we have known to date. He is also asking us to rethink the kind of learners we want an education system to produce. Put simply, is transition in the new millennium going to be a key instrument through which we create an education system that serves the person, not the other way round?

Case example three

Three schools in the UK's East Midlands, a mixed comprehensive, a high school and a primary school, share the same campus set in the middle of a much sought after middle class housing estate. There have been major concerns expressed over the timings and procedures regarding transition. Moving at Year 5, just before national standard assessment tests, has resulted in an alarming performance dip; moving at the end of Year 9 just when GCSEs are about to begin has led to significant slippage in the first term of Year 10. One school is too small, another is too large for the student cohort and the third is in a terminal state of disrepair. Following on from a joint meeting of the LEA and the schools' governing bodies, a radical solution has been proposed. The land will be sold for much needed housing development. The £37 million gained from selling the site is going to be used to build a brand new 4–18 all-through Learning Academy. In this way it is envisaged that transition is much more likely to be personalised, seamless and ultimately much more effective.

Transitional bridges

Ruth Sutton (2000), in her aptly named *Overcoming the Muddle in the Middle*, talks of the five bridges of transition:

- managerial/bureaucratic;

- social/personal;
- curriculum content/continuity;
- pedagogical;
- management of learning.

These bridges, we believe, provide a constructive platform for developing a clearer insight into what will make for effective transition in twenty-first century learning schools.

Managerial/bureaucratic

Reality dictates that no matter how innovative or revolutionary any school's aims might be, they must be underpinned by efficient and effective organisational and administrative procedures. Although there is a strong case for eliminating as much as possible of the negative consequences of moving school by creating 4–18 all-through schools like the case study already cited, the fact is that for the majority of children, existing structures will remain for the foreseeable future. Learning schools will therefore need to have at the forefront of their thinking a determination to ensure that cross-phase organisational procedures are of sufficient robustness and quality to make transition as seamless as possible. They should be determined to create strong bonds with feeder schools that impact positively on the transition process. Key objectives should be to:

- make the transfer of information as ICT efficient (i.e. paper-free!), comprehensive, relevant and as e-learning-centred as possible;
- ensure that familiarisation procedures (visits, meetings, talks) are centred on learning rather than marketing and enhancing the reputations of respective organisations;
- establish administrative mechanisms which will support teachers, parents and children through the process of change;
- ensure that communication between all parties is clear, informative, non-judgemental and two-way;
- keep bureaucracy to a minimum and personalise the transition process as much as possible.

There is no doubt that the potential for allowing transition to become a negative rather than a positive experience is significant. Each organisation will have its particular vision and culture supported by institutionally driven structural divisions. Parents and teachers may well agree on any number of issues ranging from assessment to uniform in one school only to find that the new school subscribes to a quite different set of expectations. There is no way all such potential barriers will be broken down but having in place managerial and bureaucratic procedures which are:

- transparent;

- carefully thought through;
- client-friendly;
- student-centred;

will help ensure that transition is an enjoyable and positive experience for everyone concerned.

Personal/social

There is a considerable temptation when thinking about how learning schools will look and operate in the mid/long-term to concentrate on the new technologies, the exciting new building programmes which are going on across the world, the potential for delivering learning in hitherto unimagined ways and forget that there are certain timeless truths which will be at the centre of any and all effective schools. Learners will always need the soft social skills which will enable them to meet and communicate with confidence. All schools need to invest heavily in the social capital which enables learners to appreciate:

- why learning is important;
- how learning should be utilised ;
- how people should interact with each other.

Transition will almost certainly create feelings of anxiety and apprehension. School leaders need to put in place activities which will reduce those feelings. Galton et al (1999 p.22) report:

> Induction days, when the pupils from all the feeder schools come together and spend a whole day in their new forms in the transfer school, have proved particularly successful. Children get to know pupils from other schools, find where to hang their coats, try out school dinners, meet some of their new teachers and experience taster lessons in subjects such as science and physical education where facilities are generally much better than in the feeder schools. Other activities such as open evenings, special visits to use the ICT, science and drama facilities, information booklets for parents and students are also used to make the school as familiar as possible prior to the move.

Such practice is far from revolutionary and most school leaders will doubtless identify with and be able to add to the examples cited here. What is crucial is always to remember that twenty-first century schools are working with students who will bring to the new learning environment needs, aspirations, fears and concerns which are the product of generations of social and cultural influences.

Case example four

A large mixed comprehensive school in a tough inner-city area in the UK north east had been experiencing an alarming deterioration in standards of behaviour, learning and attitudes to any form of authority on the part of a large number of the children transferring to them from neighbouring primary schools. Standards across the curriculum had nose-dived and a feeling of siege mentality had pervaded the whole school. Staff had become demoralised and fearful that the whole pastoral and academic structure of the new intake cohorts was breaking down and impacting significantly on the whole school. Three years ago the leadership group decided to take out part of the campus which was geographically self-contained and turn it into a primary school within a school. Teachers volunteered to work solely with this particular year group and the structure of the lessons, the school day and the daily routines (including having coat pegs, 'playtime' and dinner monitors) were deliberately primary focused. In this way, the children transferring to 'the big school' were gradually introduced to the new environment and went through a series of learning experiences which were far less obvious and potentially threatening. The change in the students' behaviour, attitude and approach to school life changed virtually over night.

Curriculum content/continuity

In the UK, the introduction a decade ago of the national curriculum was a formal attempt by government to make transition through the different learning phases as seamless as possible. However, like most seemingly simple solutions to a complex problem, it was too simplistic. Although the national curriculum is now firmly embedded in schools, the reality is that not all children have learned the same things and know the same amount. Children, in fact, vary enormously in how they have responded to the detail of the programmes of study and the extent to which they have grasped the concepts. This, of course, raises key questions for learning schools:

- Will twenty-first century schools be able to create a core curriculum for personalised learning?
- Will they be able to define a basic national framework to ensure that every student reaches a minimum standard?
- Will, in fact, formal corporate assessment practice be replaced by individual ICT driven pupil tracking?
- How will learning schools be able to devise programmes of study (learning pathways) that promote real and positive risk-free choices?
- How will learning schools make certain that throughout the transition process students learn how to make decisions and be centrally involved in their own assessment?

At the centre of this is the key question: to what extent will twenty-first century learning schools be able to combine best practice in curriculum development and transitional procedures to ensure that learners' needs and aspirations are always the first consideration? McCall and Lawlor (2002 p.7) suggest:

> The organisation of successful learning lies in identifying students' zones of next development (Vygotsky 1962) and then moving the learners on to the next stratum of knowledge, understanding and skill. This implies that teachers have refined skills in determining pupils' learning needs and can arrange this training so that units of work, learning activities and learning tasks are based on students' existing layers of experience.

The challenge therefore is to promote curriculum continuity alongside person-alised learning to create individual learning pathways for every student – a huge task! As Hopkins (2004 p.8) observes:

> We need to be moulding schools to the learning needs of students, rather than moulding students to schools. Key to all this is assessment for learning (see Chapter 10 of this book) and how we present teaching and learning inside our schools – and also how we open up the curriculum so it's both an opportunity for choice but also a pathway for entitlement.

It is also vital that curriculum continuity carries on within as well as across school phases. Nicholls and Gardner (1999 p.30) argue:

> Clearly before schools look at their response to ensuring continuity across the divide they must first look to ensure that they are building progressively on children's learning within their own schools… With continuity and progression being addressed within a school, understanding of what has gone on in the previous stage, and the needs of the next stage is likely to be more keenly developed.

Pedagogy

If transition is going to be an effective instrument for enhancing learning it is vital that those factors impacting on children's learning and experience are at the forefront of effective liaison between schools across the transition boundary. Nicholls and Gardner (1999 p.79) highlight:

> On transfer to a UK secondary school, pupils encounter forms of specialist teaching from say, scientists, historian or geographers which they may not have experienced previously. The difference in experience between usually having one class teacher virtually all day every day in the primary schools and perhaps as many as ten or more specialist teachers in secondary schools at different times each day, must have an impact on how pupils perceive the learning environment to which they transfer.

The following example illustrates a simple truth about transitional learning.

Case example five

In a recent Ofsted inspection of a secondary school in the south east of England a 12 year-old boy was asked about homework. He said that it was completely different from how they did things in his junior (primary) school: 'We used to study things like the Romans for a whole week. We really got into it and it was interesting. I used to enjoy reading up on it when I got home. Now we do lots of different lessons each day and then we get lots of different homework. It's not the same. Anyway, at my old school we didn't get proper homework. We just used to carry on with what we'd be doing at school during the day. It wasn't a chore. I used to enjoy it!'

Such examples illustrate a lack of continuity between the primary focus on learning and the secondary focus on subject knowledge.

Effective partnerships across phases will have teaching styles and contexts at their centre. Key strategies might be:

- organised observations of teaching in each other's schools, particularly in numeracy, literacy, science and technology;
- pupils taking part in sample lessons;
- targeted use of cross-phase video conferencing and e-mail to increase understanding of specific teaching strategies;
- developing joint programmes where pupils work in collaborative groups;
- promoting cross-phase activities aimed at improving problem-solving and thinking skills;
- positive systematic recognition of prior learning;
- shared professional development;
- teacher-to-teacher visits and observations;
- using the same books before and after transition;
- setting up bridging modules which recognise current and anticipate future learning pathways;
- regular programmes of parent, staff and student visits to cross-phase schools;
- joint curriculum activities.

All of these strategies will help teachers to understand that learners' needs do not develop in stages and that a good deal of what happens in any school is familiar to learners but a significant element is new which, in the students' eyes, may present potential threats as well as opportunities. The truth is, that for as long as schools have existed, the shape and content of the school day alongside the procedures for moving from one school to another have been designed to suit teachers rather than learners. Twenty-first century learning schools will need to recognise and acknowledge that fact and put in place strategies which will suit learners first.

Management of learning

Transition in twenty-first century learning schools will be driven by 'age' rather than 'stage'. By freeing learners from the constraints of predetermined corporate pathways and allowing them to choose how, where and what they learn, learning schools will be instrumental in encouraging schools to be proactive about their own learning. Added to that, the decisions they make on their personal journeys will be communicated to parents much more effectively and rapidly. Tarleton (2004 p.32) suggests:

> *Soon mobile phone technology might be used to update parents about grades, homework, absences, alerts or rewards, in the way that some banks are now providing customers with daily texts of updates of current accounts. This is not information for the sake of it: the organisation is providing up-to-date user-friendly information sent to the individual consumer to act upon.*

In the final analysis, transition needs to be seen not as a means to pre-existing ends, but an opportunity to provide an education system that serves and empowers the learner.

McCall and Lawlor (2001 p.21) make the following observation:

> *A crucial element of the school's support for individual students will be the degree of 'match' achieved between the nature and activities provided by the learning opportunities and students' general stages of learning development. Teachers need good awareness of students' levels of prior attainment, students' 'highs' and 'lows' with previous learning activities and their overall capacity to sustain 'time-on-task'. The latter element is one indicator of their likely engagement rate with the learning process.*

Making the change

The positive learning environment

Teachers in learning schools will need to have a clear understanding of their students' previous, current and potential learning development. This can be achieved if they have clear objectives and ask key questions, such as the following.

Objective

To see their stage in the learners' personal journey as one part of the transitional process, not a self-contained journey with a beginning and an end.

Question

What steps are taken currently in your school to convey this clear message to students, staff and parents?

Objective

To have working relationships with feeder schools that sustain effective two-way communication.

Questions

How do you currently ensure that all relevant staff are thoroughly up to date with what is going on in your feeder schools?

Is some of what you do more concerned with protocol and social networking than with learning?

Objective

To recognise and understand pupil perceptions and expectations.

Questions

Do you invest in formal and informal consultation exercises with students starting at your school?

Are they ever asked if they've done a topic that is being proposed to be covered?

Do they have the opportunity to express their initial thoughts, apprehensions, perceptions and disappointments in supportive forums?

Are they asked regularly what they think of their lessons and the programmes of study they are following?

Is their advice acted upon?

Objective

To encourage key skills which can be utilised in all the educational phases.

Questions

How much investment of time and expertise is to be put into cross-phase programmes which will equip learners with learning strategies which they can use when they transfer to a new school?

How much of the ICT infrastructure is common to all phases?

Building new relationships

Transition should provide relevant and stimulating opportunities for learners to have the confidence and the curiosity to make new friendships. Such friendships will encourage the learner as follows.

Objective

To observe how others learn and benefit in turn from experimenting with new learning styles.

Questions

Are students given time and support to grow into their new school and begin to make new friends?

Are strategies introduced which encourage them from the outset to work with students from other schools in order that they break out of the comfort zone of remaining with learners and learning styles they are familiar and safe with?

Is time built into the curriculum to allow the students to develop the self-confidence to debate issues maturely and create a sense of tolerance and understanding of the world in which they live?

Learning schools will recognise that effective learning can only take place when the learner feels secure in their working environment and that security comes primarily from a keen awareness of how the school accepts and advocates the building of relationships. McCall and Lawlor (2002 p.99) observe:

> *They will be influenced by immediate happenings prior to a lesson and by their general sense of well-being at the time the lesson takes pace. They cannot entirely divorce their reactions in a lesson from their overarching feelings about life and about the demands they have to meet outside of school.*

Emotional intelligence: making the most of the journey

Learning schools will need to utilise all the facilities available to them to ensure that their students feel motivated, challenged and liberated from any of the predetermined hurdles that have hindered individual growth for so long.

Objective

To develop sustained and effective collaborative partnerships with all feeder schools.

Questions

How far is organisational prejudice about the quality of learning that takes place in feeder schools recognised and confronted?

How keen are the staff to familiarise themselves with programmes of study which appear not immediately relevant to their own needs?

Objective

To create dynamic and properly focused opportunities for taking risk-free choices that help and encourage students to believe in themselves and make good decisions about their learning.

Question

How is it demonstrated that the school is committed to the principle of putting the learners' needs at the centre of all advice about which subjects they should study even when there is a risk of failure implicit in the decision?

Objective

To create structures which follow culture and not the other way round.

Questions

Does the school's mission statement capture what you as a learning school are concerned with or is it too focused on external demands and expectations?

Are the students clear about the ethos and culture of their school or do they have different views?

What checks are taken to discover whether they are happy, challenged and secure?

Objective

To allow flexibility of time and space to enable learners to grow.

Questions

Is enough time spent on helping learners how to learn?

Are learners encouraged to enjoy the journey just as much as the arrival at the destination?

Will all the students have a clear and accurate assessment of their own learning as they progress through the school?

Objective

To maintain and sustain, through the new technologies, ample time to access learning at times which suit the learner not just the teacher.

Question

What steps are being taken to invest in setting up procedures which will make the concept of a 24-hour school a reality?

Objective

At all times to encourage students to become leaders of their own learning.

Questions

What steps are taken to show that the school welcomes less control and more delegated responsibility to the students?

How is it conveyed that a 'good' mistake is valid learning, even if it impacts negatively on results?

How are students encouraged to criticise constructively and how is it demonstrated that their comments are noted and acted upon?

This is of course far from an exhaustive list. At the heart of these action points is a need to ensure that all learners have the will, the determination and the means to do best by their own skills and intelligence at whatever transitional stage they may be on their personal learning journey.

References

Erikson, E. (1979) *Childhood and Society*. London: Triad/Granada

Galton, M., Gray, J and Ruddock, J. (1999) *The Impact of Schools Transition and Transfers on Pupil Progress and Attainment*. London: DfES.

Gibbons, M. (2004) 'Custom built for every student', *Times Educational Supplement*; p.31, 25 June.

Hopkins, D. (2004) *Personalised Learning*, Special Leader Supplement. Nottingham: National College for School Leadership.

Leadbeater, C. (2004) *Learning about Personalisation*. London: DfES.

McCall and Lawlor (2002) *Leading and Managing Effective Learning*. London: Optimus.

Nicholls, G. and Gardner, J. (1999) *Pupils in Transition*. London: Routledge.

Sutton, R. (2000) *From Primary to Secondary: Overcoming the Muddle in the Middle*. London: RS Publications.

Tarleton, R. (2004) 'Please take this personally', *Times Education Supplement*, 25 June.

Chapter 10

Assessment for Learning

Preview

This chapter considers the following questions:

- How can we ensure that the way we assess students helps not hinders their learning?
- How can we make assessment an integral part of learning?
- Why is formative assessment so much more crucial than summative?
- How can students in the classroom understand what progress they are making?
- How can assessment for learning be integrated into the learning school ethos?

> *The trinity of assessment, teaching and learning governs everything we do. And recently I have begun to think that the key to it all is the first of these ...*
>
> Brighouse (2003)

Does assessment enhance learning?

Assessment has been used by most governments in the second half of the twentieth century as a central tool in efforts to raise standards of measurable achievement. Examination results have been used in the UK and other countries to encourage competition between schools and to identify under-achievement. However, recent evidence suggests that measuring school improvement through examination results leads to a plateau of attainment and an absence of real cognitive development that makes learning transferable. In the UK, concern about this plateau has led to greater engagement with research around more formative approaches to assessment.

> *High stakes tests always dominate both teaching and assessment. They give poor models for formative assessment.*
>
> (Black and Wiliam, 1998)

Claxton (1995) compares teaching to the test to throwing a rope into a swimming pool. The student ties it around their waist whilst the teacher runs down the side of the pool pulling as hard and fast as they can. At the end, the student has improved their time but the teacher is exhausted and the student has learnt nothing, apart from dependence. Teaching the students how to breathe correctly and improve their swimming skills and techniques takes much longer initially but eventually creates independence and long-lasting improvement in achievement.

As summative assessment has dominated education, teachers have worked harder and students have become more dependent through the latter part of the twentieth century. However, there is no doubt that assessment can and does form a crucial scaffold in embedding learning that is transferable.

The schools that are visited that are performing well or improving had all developed robust approaches to target setting and monitoring pupil progress.
(National Audit Office, November 2003)

One of the keys to raising standards effectively may depend on how teachers monitor student progress during their learning experiences. Assessment should be recognised as a powerful *formative* process rather than as a means to simply judge summative outcomes.

An excellent model of learning

A baby is highly motivated to learn to speak. It seeks constant feedback and is not afraid of making mistakes over and over again. It corrects itself constantly and tries out new methods of learning such as singing, shouting and crying – constantly. It loves praise and encouragement and usually gets it! **It never gives up** – until it gets there… If all our students followed this model they could learn anything!

Previous chapters have referred to the need for an emotionally intelligent school where students develop self-awareness and the ability to motivate themselves. Assessment falls very clearly into the EQ section of the learning school hierarchy. Reflecting on achievement, learning from mistakes and setting your own targets are all part of a formative approach to assessment that should be an integral part of the ethos and practice of all twenty-first century schools.

But how can teachers use ongoing assessment in the classroom to improve exam results and create independent, emotionally intelligent learners? This chapter aims to provide ideas about approaches to assessment in the classroom and discuss the relevance of leadership and ethos in a school where assessment really is *for* learning.

Every mistake is a learning experience – there's no such thing as failure, only feedback.

Paul Black and Dylan Wiliam (1998) of Kings College, London caused a major rethink of UK government policy on assessment with their research on raising standards through classroom assessment in *Inside the Black Box*. In their work, Black and Wiliam used the term formative assessment to encompass all those activities that provide feedback to students on their progress – i.e. self-assessment, peer assessment and teacher assessment, both written and oral. Such assessment, they say, becomes formative when the evidence is actually used to adapt 'the teaching work to fulfil the needs.'

Their research was international and drew on educational expertise from Australia, France, Hong Kong, South Africa and the USA. The conclusions were that:

- such formative assessment can and does raise standards of achievement;
- there is room for improvement in standards of formative assessment in schools;
- there is evidence about how to improve formative assessment.

Black and Wiliam (1998) found that :

All studies show that innovations which include strengthening the practice of formative assessment produce significant and often substantial learning gains.

These studies were not limited to a particular context, but ranged from 5 year olds to undergraduates, from history to maths and from the USA to Hong Kong. The studies also demonstrated that improved formative assessment helps the low attainers more than the rest, and so 'reduces the spread of attainment whilst also raising it overall.' Significant changes in classroom practice and modes of pedagogy are indicated by the research. These are entirely congruent with the learning ethos described in previous chapters of this book that:

- students must be actively involved in their own learning;
- teachers must be flexible and make adjustments to teaching and learning according to student needs;
- consideration must be given to the motivation and self-esteem of students as they become engaged in self-assessment.

Common practice in assessment

Black and Wiliam (1998) found that:

- marking is usually conscientious but often fails to offer guidance on how work can be improved;
- teachers' tests encourage rote and superficial learning; this is seen even where teachers say they want to develop understanding – and many seem unaware of this inconsistency;

- the giving of marks and the grading are over-emphasised whilst the giving of useful advice and the learning function are under-emphasised;
- assessment feedback teaches pupils with low attainment that they lack 'ability', so they become demotivated;
- teachers' feedback to pupils seems to serve social and managerial functions at the expense of learning;
- teachers know too little about their pupils' learning needs;
- the collection of marks in the records is given greater priority than analysis of the pupil's work to discern learning needs.

The above reflect a historical tendency to teach, and hope that students would learn without sight of the criteria for grading or of sample exam papers. We are now developing our knowledge of the brain and moving away from ideas of fixed inherited intelligence towards a belief that every child is capable of greater achievement. This is supported by an acceptance of the ideas (as in Chapter 7) about varying approaches according to learning styles and multiple intelligences. The belief is underpinned by the necessity for a whole school approach to a culture that sees mistakes as opportunities to learn. Assessment for learning is a crucial part of this paradigm shift in thinking.

How to improve formative assessment in the classroom

The aim in the learning school for the twenty-first century is to develop a love of learning for its own sake – an intrinsic enjoyment of the process of the acquisition of skills and knowledge that can be energising and motivating. There is no doubt that all students want to experience success and need to know how to succeed, but as learning is predominantly an emotional experience it is crucial for the learner to receive ongoing feedback that is clear and constructive throughout the learning process.

Learning takes place in a cognitive context, proposed by Dubin (1962) and referred to in Chapter 2, where we become conscious of our 'incompetence' as we begin the learning process. At this point we face stress and the temptation to give up. It is here that we need the optimum feedback and support. It is here that our self-esteem is most at risk and the quality of our emotional intelligence will be sorely tested. Without the appropriate feedback during this phase we will seek to retreat to the comfort of the unconscious incompetence state. Because students too often get inappropriate assessment feedback, many decide not to try rather than risk getting it wrong.

The process of learning can be arduous but also very rewarding. Moving through these cognitive phases can be immensely satisfying – a good example of this process is something like learning to ski – it seems so easy once you can do it! *The most important difference between this process and what happens in a classroom is the lack of the constant personal adjustments made by the learner to their own progress.* In our early learning experiences, learning to walk or talk as young children, self-assessment and adjustment were intrinsic to the instinctive process of learning.

November, in a keynote speech for the Specialist Schools Trust 2002, suggested that computer games are the ultimate self-assessment learning experience. 'Game theory' suggests that when children play computer games and develop the skills required to move up levels of ability, they constantly set themselves higher standards and use a trial and error method of learning. The game gives instant individualised feedback and develops unconscious competence at pace.

Formative assessment can be a powerful weapon in the creation of a culture of success backed by a belief that all can achieve.

To many pupils, school appears to be a series of activities that make little sense, and they spend their time negotiating their way through these tasks with as little damage as possible to their self-esteem – they end up just 'doing school'. They are fascinated if they get a glance at the mark book, so that they can see if they are 'getting somewhere' in their learning.

As Sadler (1989) notes:

The indispensable conditions for improvement are that the student comes to hold a concept of quality roughly similar to that held by the teacher, is continuously able to monitor the quality of what is being produced during the act of production itself, and has a repertoire of alternative moves or strategies from which to draw at any given point.

For some activities, such as the decoding of a maths formula, it is relatively straightforward for a student to know whether they have achieved this or not. For other aims of learning, such as 'writing a good essay', there cannot be any hard-and-fast criteria for success, but students can be helped to develop what Claxton calls 'a nose for quality.' This nose will take years to develop but it can be developed in the learning school through a rigorous, determined approach to use formative assessment that involves students being interactive with their learning.

While it might be thought that pupils should always know what is wanted in the classroom, in fact pupils often hold quite different views of quality from the teacher. This is because, traditionally, teachers haven't shared learning goals and judgements. Students need to develop the same unconscious competence about judging their work that teachers do having closely marked dozens of exam papers.

If pupils are to become increasingly responsible for their own learning they must also be involved in their own assessment. A central message that emerged from the Black and Wiliam review (1998) was that this is something that has to be done by pupils and cannot be done for them, a point reinforced by the Assessment Reform Group (1999):

Current thinking about learning acknowledges that learners must ultimately be responsible for their learning since no one else can do it for them. Thus assessment for learning must involve pupils, so as to provide them with information about how well they are doing and guide their subsequent efforts. Much of this information will come as feedback from the teacher, but some will be through their direct involvement in assessing their own work. The awareness of learning and ability of learners to direct it for themselves is of increasing importance in the context of encouraging lifelong learning.

It is the lower achievers who are most at risk from the culture of summative assessment pervasive in the UK in the latter part of the twentieth century.

The Learn Project, set up by the Centre for Assessment Studies at Bristol University School of Education, interviewed over 200 students aged 3 to 13 on the subject of assessment and how they perceived it is used to help them improve their learning. Fifty-six of these students were identified as low achievers. This group were found to:

- be motivated emotionally by their preference for the teacher or subject;
- be concerned with performance rather than understanding – some had an attitude of 'learned helplessness';
- demonstrate a poorer understanding of assessment requirements than their peers;
- have an inconsistent understanding of what to do for individual tasks;
- depend on teacher-set standards when judging their work;
- be often confused by effort and attainment grades;
- rarely have opportunities for self-assessment;
- prefer prompt oral feedback;
- use feedback ineffectively;
- think that feedback which they felt was constructive helped their performance.

Case example one

A consultant working on raising standards of writing encouraged teachers to identify major factors limiting students' progress. They discovered that limited vocabulary and lack of reading made a major impact. Using this to plan intervention they targeted vocabulary enrichment through drama, linking it to kinaesthetic learning preferences. Using this and positive focused marking with constructive feedback the writing skills improved to create a 15 per cent increase in English results at Key Stage 2 in 2000.

Many students are afraid to ask or answer questions because they fear being wrong and embarrassed in front of peers. Those who believe they are not capable of success withdraw from the learning within the classroom and seek kudos in other ways such as disrupting the lesson. This leads to still lower achievement and the self-fulfilling prophecy of underachievement is reinforced. Quite often these students (especially boys) achieve well in sport where the coaching pedagogic method suits their style more effectively or their kinaesthetic preferences produce successful outcomes. If they could transfer their positive state of mind from the sports field to the classroom they would have the confidence to benefit from feedback.

> *Feedback to any pupil should be about the particular qualities of his or her work, with advice on what she or he can do to improve, and should avoid any comparisons with other pupils.*
>
> (Black and Wiliam, 1998)

It is students such as these who make up the bulk of young people not achieving the expected five A*–C grades at 16 years old in the UK. Their lack of success with current methods of assessment makes them prefer to stay in unconscious incompetence and opt out emotionally from the academic challenges presented by schools. An assessment regime which creates regular opportunities for success and clear evidence of achievable progress is essential for this group of learners.

Student comments from The Learn Project (University of Bristol CLIO Centre) Year 9 (age 13) students.
Students often did not see the 'big picture' of a course.
'She'd give us a booklet which tells us what we'll do. It's got marks for each bit.'
'We don't know how it will be assessed but we know what to do; they give us sheets and stuff.'
'Most of my teachers say I could improve my presentation. It's not very helpful because they've said it so many times.'

Black and Wiliam showed that large improvements in performance, particularly for low achievers, can be secured when students are helped to engage meaningfully with their own learning and given the tools to assess their own progress for themselves.

A further dimension to assessment for the twenty-first century learning school to address is a commitment to self-assessment and peer assessment alongside the provision of accurate data and comprehensible criteria about what students are meant to achieve. Research has shown students are accurate and often reliable in assessing themselves and others when given a clear picture of what the learning targets are. Another benefit of this system means that students are *given access* to this vital information. Black and Wiliam found children were used to classroom teaching as an arbitrary sequence of exercises with no rationale. When students have access to the purpose and criteria of the learning, their progress and commitment is much improved. Far from being a luxury or a lazy teacher's answer to a heavy marking load, self- and peer assessment is an 'essential component of formative assessment.'

Sadler (1989) suggested that each of the following three elements must be included and understood in good learning:

- the desired goal;
- the present position;
- what to do to close the gap.

This simple paradigm needs to be embedded in classroom practice through the strategies of self-assessment and reflective target-setting that is flexible, personalised and adaptable to change as learning progresses.

How could we change the nature of assessment used by teachers?

Diverse research studies show what is needed is to:

- train students to use self-assessment and peer assessment;
- use classroom questioning for learning and thinking;
- focus marking with specific target setting;
- share the criteria for assessment to create real understanding of how we judge progress;
- set tasks and tests that inform students about their learning;
- give immediate, clear oral and written feedback that create targets for improvement.

This section looks at the way teachers can assess student progress and how a more formative approach could assist achievement and self-esteem. The ideas are based on the research findings of Black and Wiliam and the recommendations of the Assessment Reform Group in *Assessment for Learning: Beyond the Black Box* (1999).

Self- and peer assessment

Self-assessment has been defined as:

> *the process of reflecting on past experience, seeking to remember and understand what took place and attempting to gain a clear idea of what has been learned or achieved.*

(Munby, 1989)

In self-assessment, pupils have to understand the criteria or standards that will be used to assess their work, make judgements about their work in relation to these and any feedback from the teacher and work out the implications of this for future action.

146

In addition to developing the skills of self-assessment, assessing the work of other pupils can develop confidence and understanding about assessment. The aim of peer assessment is to help pupils move forward in their learning. New learning strategies can be developed by scrutinising the work of others and being able to make a comparison with their own work. It gives pupils a wider view of what is possible.

By assessing others' work, students have the opportunity to see different ways of tackling a task and during the feedback they need to analyse the strengths and weaknesses of the effort. This embeds a deeper understanding of the learning.

Druckman and Swets (1988) argue that peer feedback is as, or more, influential than teacher feedback in obtaining lasting performance results, but as QCA (2001) suggest:

Effective learning will occur only if pupils are clear about what they know, understand and can do at the start of a piece of work and what they will know, understand and be able to do when they have completed the work.

Self- and peer assessment help pupils to become more effective learners by enabling them to reflect on:

- their knowledge of themselves as learners;
- their understanding of the task in hand;
- ways in which they can improve their learning;
- how to set their own targets for improvement.

In doing so, it contributes to increased self-esteem, motivation and personal responsibility for learning.

For self-assessment to work, it is important that pupils are given opportunities to reflect on the quality of their work against given criteria written in their language. They need to be supported to admit to difficulties without risk to their self-esteem; to accept the fundamental principle that every mistake is a learning experience – in fact that learning rarely takes place without setbacks. They need to be given time to work problems out and know that it is acceptable to consider a number of possible solutions before acting. If the principle of 'if it doesn't work try something else' is part of the school ethos, failure becomes feedback.

Case example two

A secondary school in London has experimented with self and peer assessment and found it has made an impressive difference in the students' understanding of what is required of them. All work is marked by students first and that includes an effort grade! The students are given the assessment criteria and are expected to look for ways to improve future work. 'Students have become more confident and comfortable with peer marking over time and their observations are developing a superb level of thinking,' commented the maths teacher in charge of the project.

Focused marking and feedback

Marking students' work can be a tremendous burden to teachers but its effectiveness in embedding learning has become questionable. The problems arise from the time it takes for students to receive the feedback, and the poor quality of the comments together with the use of grades which do not always offer constructive ways forward. Black and Wiliam found that students tend to focus on the grade, if there is one, to the detriment of any targets set. In their research, students were found to make more progress when given practical strategies for improvement rather than grades or levels. They also reported research in Israel that showed students who were:

- given marks only made limited progress;
- given marks and comment made limited progress;
- given developmental comment only ... made a 30 per cent increase in attainment.

Characteristics of effective feedback

The Qualifications and Curriculum Authority (2001) offers the following:

- Feedback is more effective if it focuses on the task, is given regularly and while still relevant.
- Feedback is most effective when it confirms the pupils are on the right tracks and when it stimulates correction of errors or improvement of a piece of work.
- Suggestions for improvement should act as 'scaffolding' i.e. pupils should be given as much help as they need to use their knowledge. They should not be given the complete solutions as soon as they get stuck, so that they must think things through for themselves.
- Pupils should be helped to find alternative solutions if simply repeating an explanation continues to lead to failure.
- Feedback on progress over a number of attempts is more effective than feedback on performance treated in isolation.
- The quality of dialogue in feedback is important and most research indicates that oral feedback is more effective than written feedback.
- Pupils need to have the skills to ask for help and the ethos of the school should encourage them to do so.

In the learning school, teacher marking may be less frequent, more focused and clearly related to setting targets for individual improvement that are understood and reviewed.

Questioning

One important finding of Black and Wiliam's (1998 p.9) review of research on formative assessment was that:

> *A particular feature of the talk between teacher and pupils is the asking of questions by the teacher. This natural and direct way of checking on learning is often unproductive. One common problem is that, following a question, teachers do not wait long enough to allow pupils to think out their answers. When a teacher answers his or her own question after only two or three seconds and when a minute of silence is not tolerable, there is no possibility that a pupil can think out what to say.*
>
> *There are then two consequences. One is that, because the only questions that can produce answers in such a short time are questions of fact, these predominate. The other is that pupils don't even try to think out a response. Because they know that the answer, followed by another question, will come along in a few seconds, there is no point in trying. It is also generally the case that only a few pupils in a class answer the teacher's questions. The rest then leave it to these few, knowing that they cannot respond as quickly and being unwilling to risk making mistakes in public. So the teacher, by lowering the level of questions and by accepting answers from a few, can keep the lesson going but is actually out of touch with the understanding of most of the class. The question/answer dialogue becomes a ritual, one in which thoughtful involvement suffers.*

The above is a familiar picture of a traditional approach to pedagogy. It is important that we develop new practice that makes questioning an integral part of learning.

The characteristics of effective questioning

The purpose of questions in the classroom should be to:

- extend thinking skills;
- clarify understanding;
- gain feedback on progress;
- provide revisions and review strategies;
- create connections;
- enhance curiosity;
- provide challenges.

Some excellent lessons contain examples of discussion as the teacher shares knowledge with the students. The teacher asks a question hoping for a certain answer that forms part of their teaching plan. Black and Wiliam found that many teachers look for a certain answer and lack the flexibility or confidence to deal with the unexpected, so they try to direct the students to the expected answer. In this way the teacher can seal off any unusual, and often thoughtful, unorthodox attempts by the pupil to work out their own answers. The object of the exercise is to guess what the teacher expects to see or hear – the conventional ritual of question and answer adds nothing to the learning experience.

The way to break this cycle is to give students thinking time. They can discuss the answer in pairs or small groups so that the respondent is answering on behalf of others and the stakes are consequently less high. The rest of the class can make judgements about the best answers and give reasons. This encourages dialogue and reflection to allow the formative learning to take place in a low risk setting where *all* students have a part to play in exploring understanding. The next stage is to encourage students to develop their own questions for planning and self-assessment; this becomes an excellent homework task especially as an understanding of higher-order questions and answers develops and students can create questions that move through levels of understanding. This task has the added bonus of providing a classroom activity where students are engaged in setting each other questions and having to form their own criteria for marking the answers!

Case example three

A school in Thame has been trialling various methods of formative assessment with impressive results. They have been using open-ended questions with sufficient wait times to make the students think. The thinking leads to group discussion and group answers. Good discussion then takes place about which answers are right and wrong and how they know. Students are encouraged to interrogate each other's answers – this helps embed the learning. They have also increased the usual answer 'wait' time to three seconds and found a huge increase in the numbers of students responding. Wrong answers are highly valued as they are used to help identify and deepen learning.

Formative tests

Instruction and formative assessment are indivisible.

(Black and Wiliam, 1998).

Tests can provide excellent feedback, frequent short ones are better than infrequent long ones. New learning should be tested a week or so after learning as this will top up knowledge and embed learning. Students can and should set and mark their own and each other's tests to develop a clear understanding of what makes a right and wrong answer. They should be encouraged to make concluding comments about how to improve.

Marks or grades alone have been shown not to be beneficial as they lead to continuous low expectation and the lack of commitment to try. The tests must produce specific guidance on strengths and weaknesses without any overall marks. Tests should come in the middle of a programme of study to check learning and create targets for development. A test at the end of a module is pointless as it's too late to work on mistakes or problems. Learning aims of the tests etc should be made clear to pupils. Perhaps teachers should ask themselves each week: 'Do I know enough about how my students are doing?'

Choice of tasks

These need to be developmental and have assessment opportunities built in, including homework and marking. Then feedback and development need to follow in response to the assessments. Opportunities need to be provided for students to reflect on their learning orally and in a written format, setting their own targets that are monitored by themselves and their teacher.

The dialogue between the student and teacher is crucial and time for this needs to be built into the curriculum. Practical suggestions for this type of activity include having a learning log and a target setting section within the exercise book. Students fill in these weekly whilst teachers move around the classroom discussing them.

Making the change

The classroom learning environment

- Establish a classroom ethos of trust and belief in everyone's ability to achieve.
- Display the assessment criteria clearly on walls and in books and refer to them frequently.
- Give the big picture of the learning and how it will be assessed through the lesson objectives.
- Ensure there are clear, shared expectations about the presentation of work.
- Make exemplar work available that shows processes as well as a finished graded product.

Classroom relationships

Teachers need to:

- Try to model the above – being self-reflective with students and producing well-presented board work.
- Try to provide oral as well as written feedback whenever possible.
- Give feedback immediately. Feedback has less impact the further away from the task it becomes. It must be constructive not just positive: *You need to …*
- Praise and celebrate achievement as frequently as possible.

Emotional intelligence – developing self-awareness and resilience in learning

- Students should be trained in self-assessment, using criteria written in language they can understand. This may take some time.
- Encourage responsible peer assessment using assessment criteria to include comments and targets for improvement.
- Encourage feedback from students about what they have learnt *every lesson*.
- Plan questions into the lesson and try to make sure there is thinking time for questions.
- Get more students involved in answering by having paired or group discussions on questions.
- Share answers and vote on the best answer giving reasons for choices.
- Identify next steps to learning with students. Encourage them to keep a learning log – a diary of thoughts about their learning progress.
- Use focused feedback to help set targets in small steps which relate to the next level of achievement. Record these targets in books and return to them regularly for updates.
- Evaluate progress and adjust teaching plans as a result of formative assessment.

Engagement using learning styles

- Use a variety of methods of assessment to suit learning styles.

Leadership and management

- Create a whole-school policy for formative assessment, linking it to summative assessment data and whole-school target setting.
- Share the policy with governors, staff and students.
- Appoint an assessment co-ordinator to lead staff development of assessment for learning practice.
- Train all staff in the value of assessment for learning and provide ongoing examples of good practice (see reflective questions as the starting point for teacher training).
- Review the impact and value of traditional subject-based parents' evenings and reports.
- Use progress review days to encourage form tutors to use data and summative assessment to set targets for the year. Facilitate further monitoring interviews with individual students to review targets within the academic year.
- Produce planners for students that include learning logs and target sheets for formative assessment.

References

Assessment Reform Group (1999) *Assessment for Learning: Beyond the Black Box.* Cambridge: University of Cambridge School of Education.

Black, P. and Wiliam, D. (1998) *Inside the Black Box: Raising Standards through Classroom Assessment.* London: King's College London School of Education. Available at: http://www.kcl.ac.uk/depsta/education/publications/blackbox.html

Brighouse, D. (2003) at DfES Advanced Skills Teachers Conference.

Claxton, G. (1995) 'What kind of learning does self-assessment drive? Developing a "nose" for quality: comments on Klenowski', *Assessment in Education: Principles, Policy and Practice*, 2(3), pp. 339–343.

Druckman, D. and Swets, J. (1988) *Enhancing Human Performance.* Washington: DC: National Academy Press.

Dubin, R. (1962) Self-*Concepts and Training Potential.* London: Pan Books.

Munby, S. (1989) *Assessing and Recording Achievement.* Oxford: Blackwell.

National Audit Office (2003) 'Making a difference – performance of maintained secondary schools in England', HC1332 session 2002–3 28 Nov. 2003. London: Stationery Office.

Paul, R. (1993) *Critical Thinking: How to Prepare Students for a Rapidly Changing World.* Santa Rosa, CA: Foundation for Critical Thinking.

QCA (2001) *Using Assessment to Raise Achievement in Mathematics: Key Stages 1, 2 and 3.* London: QCA. Available at: http://www.qca.org.uk/ca/5-14/afl/afl_maths.pdf

Sadler, R. (1989) 'Formative assessment and the design of instructional systems', *Instructional Science*, 18, pp.119–144.

University of Bristol (2002) The Learn Project, Bristol CLIO Centre, University of Bristol.

Chapter 11

The Role of Parents in the Learning School

Preview

This chapter considers the following questions:

- **Why is it essential for schools to get parents involved?**
- **How can they be supported and developed as learners?**
- **How can schools make more of what parents have to offer?**
- **How can schools engage those in disadvantaged contexts?**

> *In these exam-crazy times, it is easy for parents to forget that the purpose of education is to create happy and fulfilled adults, not exam fodder. If they make their love conditional upon performance, it is a recipe for depression.*
>
> Oliver James (2004)

Why involve parents?

There are three very important reasons why a school should pay particular attention to engaging parents in its development and its activities. The term 'parents' used throughout this chapter is used for simplification, and is meant to include absent parents, step parents, foster parents and, where appropriate, grandparents, carers and anyone who involves themselves with a school to support a particular child.

First, parents are indisputably the most important stakeholders that a school has, for the simple reason they provide the children – no children, no school!

Secondly, parents are the first educators of children. They influence children's first stages of learning, from birth to 3 years, which are recognised as the most significant in a human's life. Furthermore, they continue to be linked with the person after he or she has completed formal schooling.

Thirdly, the evidence from research over long periods has consistently shown that parental involvement and support makes a significant impact on pupil achievement and progress. Desforges's review (2003) of the many studies in the field confirmed this impact. The more crucial question therefore is *how* are parents best engaged in the learning school?

Rationale for parental engagement in the learning school

One of the factors that has hindered greater parental involvement in schools has been parents' fear that they did not know enough of what was being taught in their children's classes to enable them to help them at home. The excellent work of most primary schools in drawing parents (especially mothers) into the process of their children's learning to read has been the outstanding exception to this. At one level, it has been appropriate for parents to respect the expert professional's technical and specialist knowledge and allow them to manage that, just as one expects other professionals to have expert knowledge in their fields of medicine, law, etc. On the other hand, many parents have felt baffled and frustrated when they are full of positive intentions to support the school in supporting their children because they feel ignorant. Remarks such as, 'I don't know how to help him with his maths – it's so different from what I did at school' or 'I know nothing about what she's doing in science' will sound familiar to both parents and teachers.

Hard as some schools have tried to get parents to see that it is support of a different kind that is needed (encouraging, positive environment, praise – 'pastoral' rather than 'academic'), many parents have felt a certain helplessness, especially in the secondary years of schooling (see Middlewood, 1999). All this is because of the focus upon *content*.

By focusing on learning as a *process* in the learning school, the opportunities for parents to relate to their son's or daughter's experience as school increase significantly. The learning school is based upon the notion that everyone connected with the school is a learner, therefore: *parents as learners can empathise with their children.*

Through this greater empathy, the parent is more likely to:

- understand better their child's learning experience;
- support better their child's own learning at school;
- be able to learn with their child;
- form a more fruitful part of the 'learning triad' (Coleman, 1998): student, parent and teacher.

Furthermore, with the extra confidence gained through parents seeing themselves as learners, the overall dialogue between home and school is likely to improve as parents have clearer understanding of what the school is trying to achieve. Given that this is also likely to bring enhanced empathy with – and occasionally sympathy for (!) – school staff, parents can be involved in a more rewarding partnership for learning with the school.

'Partnership' is the word most commonly used to describe relationships between home and school. The OECD report (1997) *Parents as Partners in Schooling* noted the range of attitudes of parents towards schools in those countries where research was carried out, pointing out how much these were rooted in the cultural and traditional origins of education in a particular country.

Unlike Denmark, for example, where the home was seen as the 'natural' educator, the UK and the USA were towards the other end of the partnership continuum with their emphasis on education as part of consumerism, and therefore a perception of parents as customers for what was provided.

Supporting the parent as learner

What are the fields of learning which parents might focus on? We suggest there are three main ones:

(a) Their own learning to learn – 'What kind of learner am I?' 'How do/can I best learn?'
(b) Child development – understanding what is involved in the various stages of early life, toddler age, junior period, adolescence, young adulthood.
(c) Learning about what is occurring at the child's school.

Considering that parents have their own adult lives and relationships to run, both family and working, we do not underestimate the demands placed upon them, but reiterate that understanding oneself as a learner will actually enlighten and alleviate some of these pressures. Books giving advice to parents stress the need to be supportive of schools and we agree with those such as Lucas and Smith (2004) who see the main job of a parent 'as fostering a love of learning!' However, that fostering will be easier for the parent and more convincing for the child if the parents themselves have their own love of learning. If not, the child will at some point question the wish of a parent for them to be enthusiastic about something. Neither of the following will convince a child that their parent really has his/her heart in *their* learning:

'I loved *Jane Eyre* when I was at school; I can't see why you don't.'
'I don't understand that subject myself, but I'm sure it's very important.'

(a) Parents' own learning

What are ways in which schools can help parents in learning about themselves as learners?

Case example one

A school in a London borough, which planned to group its students on entry (Year 7) by learning styles, invited their parents to undertake the same VAK quiz as their sons and daughters – with the language slightly adapted. This was an exercise designed to:

- reassure the parents that the groupings did not penalise anyone;
- explain the reasoning and background behind learning styles;
- show that the groupings did not depend upon a *test*;
- get the parents interested in learning as a process by thinking of themselves as having their own way of learning.

The last of these worked in a way beyond the school's expectations. Some students complained their parents became far too interested! The initial take up of parents was about 55 per cent but, as word spread that it was not a test of parental intelligence, the figure rose to 85 per cent. (The quiz could be done at home or at school.) Parents were naturally interested in family traits and gender patterns, and the school was obliged to organise two evening workshops at which staff, parents and students discussed the process and the implications.

Most of all, these parents were drawn into dialogue about learning and what the school could do to utilise knowledge of styles to encourage achievement.

The encouragement through formal processes – offered informally – to parents to view themselves as learners is one way in which schools can help.

The overriding way is, as the school in the above case study found, through dialogue between parents and staff, between students and parents about learning. As Chapter 10 on assessment for learning described, the need is for parents to be constantly asking not 'how many marks did you get?' but 'what did you learn?' This has significant implications for the way in which schools inform parents about their children's progress – school reports – to which they have a statutory right.

(b) Child development

Parents learn a great deal about child development through their own children's development and the development of friends' and relatives' children. There is no suggestion that school staff, many of whom will not be parents and therefore not have that personal experience, know more or know better by virtue of their role. Many parents however do look to schools for advice and school staff will be better read and trained than some parents, since most of them will have had an element of child development as part of their formal training.

Learning schools can support this element of parents' learning by, for example:

- Providing relevant formal programmes on site for parents and potential parents. These ideally will be offered by experts in medicine, psychology, welfare, and not by educationalists. Indeed such programmes may benefit from teachers and other school staff attending with students' parents.
- Offering aspects of child development within the curriculum on offer.

- Facilitating opportunities for parents and future parents to work in temporary placements in nurseries, youth groups etc.
- Arranging seminars and workshops in which parents of children of different ages share experiences and strategies.
- Arranging workshops for parents on a topic which is prominent at any one time in the school. For example, an outbreak of antisocial behaviour could lead to a workshop for parents on their role in this. What is to be avoided is the summoning of parents to a school and hectoring them (or so it is perceived) on their duties. Rather, it is an opportunity to explore the issues.
- Exploring what are appropriate strategies for a particular age group. Thus, a workshop on 'rewards and praise for adolescents' would help those parents to work out their individual approaches in an understood context of appropriateness.

Case example two

In an attempt to help parents be appropriately supportive of their sons and daughters who were revising for public examinations at 16 plus, one school surveyed all parents of that age group to ascertain what kind of issues faced them. Having analysed the data, interviews with a sample of parents were held and recommendations included:

- letters about revision would go jointly to parents and students;
- an annual evening (with workshops) would be held for parents and students just prior to a period of revision;
- a network of students in groups in villages where they lived was established, with parents taking it in turns to host a group of four or five students doing revision together.

A review after one year showed many parents reported improved relationships with their children during what is a tense period with, as one parent noted, 'a much better balance of nagging and saying nothing' being achieved!

(c) Learning about what happens at school

This is the area where most schools rightly feel that they already do a great deal. However, the physical presence of parents in schools is still commonly the criterion by which some schools make judgements about the extent of parental interest. As Beresford and Hardie (1996) pointed out, this has disadvantages for some parents and more emphasis needs to be placed on a wide range of strategies to develop accessible two-way communication. Developing technology has made some of these strategies possible.

> ## Case example three
>
> Three subject departments in a school in Walthamstow, London, established e-mail networks for students taking their subjects and also involved their parents. Examples from the business studies department included:
>
> - asking parents if they knew of local businesses that might be used in students' case studies;
> - asking parents if they could suggest good examples of local retailers responding to customer complaints or requests;
> - using parents to 'test out' local companies' services, enabling case examples to emerge for their children;
> - inviting parents to hear their children read a paper to them prior to class presentation, not for content, but for preparation and confidence;
> - inviting parents to role play e.g. employer/employee situations.

All three departments extended this into giving parents feedback on the work by thanking them and telling them how the role play went.

None of this involved the parents setting foot in the school but it utilised parents' daily experiences as a shopper, customer, employee, etc, making them feel this is relevant to their son's or daughter's learning at school and valuing their own contribution to this.

Schools learning from parents

Whilst schools have been seen as the professional base for learning, the role of the parents has been to assume the role of supporting the school in its task. With a subtle change in emphasis, with everyone – including parents – being perceived as learners, schools have to acknowledge what it is that parents can potentially bring to the learning partnership.

Whilst teachers bring professional expertise, their training and experience, specialist knowledge, skills in the craft of teaching, and knowledge of the system of formal education, parents bring some things which are essential to the child's learning effectively. These include:

- intimate personal knowledge of the whole child;
- knowledge about the child before formal schooling began;
- awareness of the child's behaviour and life outside of school;
- a strong emotional attachment;
- an awareness that they have a life-long commitment and relationship;
- opportunities to help the child learn in quite literally the 'real' world;
- values, beliefs and attitudes of their own home.

Schools have traditionally been poor at acknowledging what parents can bring to the learning partnership. For example, the emotional support that parents can give to children can be very significant and yet for many parents and children the only times that the school contacts them is when there is a problem. One headteacher, introducing a scheme by which a staff member telephoned parents just to let them know that all was progressing well at school and to see if there were any issues the school ought to know about, reported that the first times this was done, the parents' automatic reaction to being told it was someone from the school was 'what's the matter?'

One of the authors has suggested elsewhere (Middlewood, 1999, p.123) that the school staff-parent relationship, as with other professional-lay person relationships, may have a number of aspects to it and sometimes these may be stages to be worked through (see Figure 11.1).

However, school professionals need to increasingly recognise the value of what parents can offer to the pupil's learning instead of seeing them as acquiescent supporters of the school's role. Some of the proactive ways in which this could be done may include (under the guidance of the school staff):

- parent and child learning together;
- parent learning from child;
- child learning from parent.

Parent and child learning together

There are many examples of all age learning groups so that we know the potential for effectiveness exists, but the emotional involvement of parents and children makes this a sensitive area. The most obvious area is perhaps that of a new topic on the curriculum where both partners come to the topic with no previous experience, and therefore no inferiority or superiority stances being taken. Beginning a new language may serve as a good example, where 'all ignorance is equal' and the practising of a few words, then phrases, then dialogue would offer both partners opportunities and even positive competition occasionally – 'who remembers the most words?'

The expert teacher will correct on accent and grammar (via class or video or compact disc contact) but the parent is a co-learner here not a teacher or tester. Any topic with a sociological or similar basis may require more time for the parent to resist asserting their superior knowledge because of their greater experience, but the parent *as learner* should be able to develop this.

Parent learning from child

The obvious example here is probably that of new technology. Most adults of at least middle age today are well aware of how children and young people see what were once new technologies, such as mobile phones and digital cameras, as a normal and to them 'obvious' part of their lives. Each new generation of children knows more than the previous one in their ever changing field and

Figure 11.1 *Managing the professional/parent relationship (Middlewood 1999).*

A *Information level*
  Process: The professional reports: the parent receives – and can also give own information.

  Outcome: Information (e.g. on child's progress at school) is held by both partners.

B *Explanation level*
  Process: The professional explains: the parent receives.

  Outcome: The parent has opportunity to ask (e.g. how and why something is taught in the way it is).

C *Observation level*
  Process: The professional performs: the parent observes.

  Outcome: The parent does not rely on words but sees school and child in action (e.g. open days/evening, visits, etc).

D *Participation level*
  Process: The professional performs: the parent is involved in performance.

  Outcome: The parent has opportunity to work in the school, be involved and both parties have some understanding of other's perception (e.g. voluntary support activity, guest speaking, etc at assemblies or to classes).

E *Consultation level*
  Process: The professional asks for opinion; the parent gives opinion.

  Outcome: The parent is consulted before a decision is made (e.g. over school uniform).

F *Negotiated level*
  Process: The professional proposes: the parent modifies proposal.

  Outcome: A debate occurs so that the final decision is more satisfactory to both (e.g. over action to be taken concerning child's behaviour).

G *Shared decision-making level*
  Process: The professional shares opinion: the parent shares opinion.

  Outcome: Both parties share in decision-making (e.g. over certain curriculum matters, school organisation and policies).

there will be many, if not most, families in which adolescent children can demonstrate to at least one parent how a new technological development operates. The patience and instructional skills needed for a child to do this are in themselves of course invaluable.

This is because the difference between the adult parents and the children here is not so much in the skills but in a mindset. To many children, the newest technological 'tool' or 'toy' is not something to be consciously learned, it is just there! To many adults, it requires a conscious learning exercise.

Child learning from parent

With the focus on learning as process, the parent need not fear ignorance of content but can help the child to learn the importance of, for example:

- coping with getting something wrong;
- sticking at something instead of giving up;
- being willing to seek help and finding out where to get it from.

Research which has been carried out into effective learning of those children who are educated at home (Meighan, 2001) can be relevant and helpful, as it is the parents who are the teachers there. The research found, among other things, that:

- working with siblings facilitated effective learning for all involved;
- a quiet place for study was *not* a key factor – the kitchen at home often came to be the natural learning zone, as the hub of activity for many families;
- working with other children – and in their homes – was an effective way of giving variety and boosting learning.

Also, the research showed that children educated at home, far from being penalised socially, were if anything better at social intercourse than many school attenders.

The relevance of all this is to challenge a traditional notion that parents must provide a quiet place of study for their children to carry out the school's tasks. Our knowledge about effective learning environments tells us that some people learn best when surrounded by noise and activity, some in quiet isolation, some by chatting to others. As Briggs (2001, p.187) emphasises, the environment needs to enable the learner to 'tune in to' learning and thus 'the learner feels respected, and feels that their needs have been assessed and acknowledged.'

We have stressed that each of the above ways in which schools can make use of what parents have to offer needs the guidance and support of the school staff. In the learning school, the staff will continually emphasise the importance of all learning outside of school, including at home, and that what parents can offer has value. It is different from what staff offer but it has a value of its own. Part of the student's development in learning for life is to assess relative values and usefulness of types of learning, contexts for learning and those in 'teaching' roles, and the differing but mutually supportive roles of school and home in this are fundamental at this crucial stage of their lives.

Learners and parents in disadvantaged contexts

It would be naïve to assume that all students have parents and homes where the kinds of support and processes described so far in this chapter can operate. A significant number of students exist in contexts outside of school where some of these ideas are alien and practices impossible. Indeed, for schools in severely disadvantaged areas of deprivation and impoverishment, such students may be the majority. Talking with staff in such schools, one is struck by the number of times they refer to the school being in fact the 'haven' for the student in a life which is otherwise disturbed and troubled, and where for them examination results seem an irrelevance. However, they also know that low achievement in those terms can mean low aspirations beyond school and the cycle of under-achievement in life can be perpetuated. (The learning school in such contexts will need to adopt specific strategies to ensure that their students are not even more disadvantaged in this way.)

Possible barriers to parental involvement

The biggest obstacle to overcome is definitely *parental perceptions of formal education and schools*, embodied in such comments as:

- *School is a waste of time. Getting into the real world and earning money and a living is what life is about.*
- *Schools are bureaucratic institutions. Like the police, the social welfare services, hospitals, they are places you only visit when you are forced to. They complain a good deal and ask you to fill in lots of forms.*
- *There is enough to worry about (job, money, etc) without having to fuss about school and what happens there.*
- *It's the teacher's job to get on with the children's learning. They don't want you sticking your nose in their business.*

These are all virtually verbatim quotations that the authors of this book have heard from parents with children at school. They indicate:

- distrust, even fear, of schools;
- suspicion of, even hostility towards the business of schooling;
- extremely low self-esteem.

How is it possible for learning schools to overcome some of these attitudes and perceptions so that these parents can be drawn into being engaged? As noted earlier, the emphasis on learning as a process is in itself a huge step forward but many parents need to be drawn in before they can understand and empathise with this. Most of the attitudes above spring from parents' own experiences of their own (particularly secondary) education which many see as having brought them failure and consequently contributed in some way to their current deprivations.

The first essential step for those working in learning schools is to *know their specific community*. It is not uncommon for schools, especially inner city ones, to organise mini-bus tours of the school's locality for all newly appointed staff prior to starting work at the school. Some even do this at the potential appointment stage. The more enlightened schools do this not in a conventional 'tour' sense.

Case example four

One headteacher of a large secondary school in a London borough of extreme deprivation describes what happens:

We take all new staff on a full day – half day at least – round our area in a mini-bus. The vehicle has the school name on the side so there's nothing covert – the staff will find out how the school is perceived. At least two current staff accompany them, ones who live in the area, one teacher, one assistant. The bus goes down every street. Where it can't get through, they get out and walk for a while. The trip includes a stop for a snack at a local fast food or even 'greasy spoon' place! It's a sensible balance – if they (especially the NQTs) are not to be voyeurs – they're there to see something of the conditions that our students and their parents live in. They hear a range of languages, including some ripe stuff! They also can meet police, wardens, shopkeepers etc. I've never had one person come back saying 'I don't want to work here.' They don't pontificate about weak parents either.

I ought to do it more for existing staff because conditions do change over time.

A good deal of statistical information is available to schools today on the socio-economic composition of the school's locality and its population but this does not get close to the actual circumstances of individual parents and their daily lives. The scale and complexity of the sociological issues involved here are way beyond the scope of one part of this single chapter, but an example of a strategy to engage parents arising from community audits and analysis may help. The emphasis is on targeting *specific* parental groups.

Step One

An analysis of a school's locality and population composition, including school records, suggests that a significant number of parents may be lone women, most of whom have low literacy and numeracy levels and many of whom are living in poverty (terms as taken from EOC, 2003).

Step Two

Ensure that these parents are offered opportunities to taste success for themselves, e.g. adult literacy classes – presentation of certificates for achievement.

Ensure groups are homogeneous (all female) – the 'We're all in the same boat' ethos can be crucial.

Ensure that opportunities exist for these to be off-site, i.e. not at school, but at local community centres for example and at times when children are at school. The idea of learning separately from their children but at the same time can be a small but significant step. The mini-bus (see above) can be used to collect mothers with transport problems. The no-cost aspect is important!

Step Three

Perhaps at the same centre, a session on how to support their own children's learnings – as already discussed.

Step Four

Invitations to the actual school, perhaps for adult classes, group meetings etc, perhaps for curriculum sessions where this is a specific emphasis on the female contribution to learning. Once the engagement has begun, any arguments about stereotyping etc can be faced.

Step Five

Step five is of course employment in some capacity linked with the school. The increasing diversity of school staff (discussed elsewhere in detail) is a rich opportunity to draw a range of people such as these in and, as some schools in deprived areas have found, it is these support staff who provide the crucial links with, knowledge of and insights into the local community so vital for developing that seamlessness between a school and its stakeholders. As the headteacher quoted above remarked:

> *If there's an incident occurring almost anywhere in the area, there's someone working here who knows all about what went on.*

No strategy will achieve everything but anything which reduces inherent tensions between parents and schools will bring benefits to parents, learners and schools. Equally significantly, such actions increase the chances that the next generation of parents will have a view of education that is more about success and enjoyment than about failure. It is this kind of long-term view to which learning schools are committed.

Making the change

Environment

Many if not most schools have focused much attention on improving their reception areas/foyers etc, making them more attractive and welcoming to visitors. They do this on the correct assumption that first impressions are crucial and for public relations the school needs to be seen as friendly as well as well organised. It takes an adjustment of a mindset to see parents not so much as visitors but as essential, integral and regular contributors to the school's wellbeing and progress.

- Do parents always have to use the official main entrance? Could a parents' entrance be created? We are conscious of the need for security of course so this entrance would need to be staffed, like any other.
- Could this entrance be, after a period, staffed by parents themselves, when they have been trained in the procedures? Whichever entrance is used, the atmosphere needs to be welcoming:
  - Does your entrance have a board or video screen welcoming today's visitors to the school *by name*?
  - Are there displays of work by students immediately visible?
  - Is there music playing in the background? Is some of this composed and/ or presented by the school's learners?
  - Have reception staff been *trained* in their roles: eye contact, body language and smiles as well as what to say?
  - Has the school got or given thought to a parents' room or area? What facilities should it have? Tea/coffee/water refreshments? Reading material? Display space for notices re events and also achievements, news etc? Internet access availability? Do the parents have responsibility for running this themselves, including payments, tidiness, etc?
  - What are the general guidelines for staff going to this area or parents going to the staff area? How have these been arrived at?
  - What are the arrangements for car parking for parents? Are they classed as visitors? Do they take their chances? How are those who live nearby encouraged *not* to use a vehicle and others to share one?

Relationships

- What structured as well as informal opportunities are in place for parents to be listened to? Suggestions box? Where? A mutual one for parents *and* staff?
- Dissatisfaction will occur from clients of any organisation. A complaint should be seen as a signal and an opportunity for the service providers to learn. Of course, style and manner is everything! The crucial thing is for those dissatisfied people to know that the school will handle the issue consistently whomever in the school it is addressed to, so that small complaints do not become big ones by having to be channelled through a long series of bureaucratic procedures.

Case example five

One school in Leicestershire developed its own code for staff in 'dealing with dissatisfaction'.

1. Respond immediately (note this does not mean 'solve it'!).
2. Thank the complainant!
3. Do not try to win an argument (because that means there is a loser).
4. Establish what you *do* agree on.
5. Explain any rules as being for the benefit of the complainant.
6. Set a time plan for getting back – and resolution if possible.
7. Sum up positively ('I'm glad we've agreed …').
8. Stay in touch.
9. Check on the situation – at school and with parent – after a period of time (do not *assume* all is well).
10. Do the whole thing with style!

- Are the school arrangements for enabling parents to discuss their children's progress: – convenient to parents (time, place)?
  – accessible?
  – comprehensible?
- Is the school ensuring that it is not judging parents as 'not caring' because they don't *physically* visit the school?
- Do parents have ample opportunity to contribute their views? How? E-mail? Home visits?
- Do all meetings between staff and parents about student progress begin with *staff asking parents* how their son/daughter appears to be progressing, attitude to school etc?

Emotional intelligence

- Do the staff empathise with the parents' role and how do they show this?
- Why not show your school values parental contribution to student learning by putting up a large chart (possibly in a parent area, but it could be elsewhere). This chart shows what staff feel they brought to the students' education. Parents are invited to write up what they feel they bring. After a while, the summary could be formalised and then updated (Figure 11.2 shows an example).
- What strategies does the school employ to help the staff who need resilience for the student's sake in those cases where parents are apathetic, unco-operative or hostile?

Figure 11.2 *What parents and staff bring to the partnership for child's learning.*

Parents bring:		Staff bring:
• Context for relevant learning • Small classes! • Lifelong commitment • Emotional attachment • Values of the home • Commitment to own development • Pride in achievement of child • Intimate knowledge of child from birth • Opportunity for family/sibling learning • Experience of child outside of school etc.	C H I L D	• Training and qualifications • Specialist knowledge – of subject and child development • Expertise in teaching and support • Awareness of school values and ethos • Belief in value of education • Professional commitment to student success • Pride in the school • Understanding of educational system • Commitment to personal learning etc.

Engagement

- What market research does the school carry out to discover the personal interests of parents, so that what is offered in extra-curricular activities can reflect those, linked with students' activities?
- Has this research revealed skills and interests which could be used by staff in their classrooms? (Demonstrating that expertise exists everywhere as well as raising the esteem of parents in the students' eyes.)
- Can smaller scale events be organised and parents with the relevant interests be encouraged to attend, eg for art exhibitions, drama, science workshops?
- Can such events be organised involving the work of *both* students and parents?
- Try an open day in which parents sample classes of learning together with students (this could lead to such classes in reality).
- Also try sample lessons with parents as a class of 12 or 15-year olds, for example, where they experience what it is like for their sons and daughters.
- Offer opportunities for parents to do their own Multiple Intelligence or VAK diagnostic quizzes, and then enable them to discuss these with staff.

Finally, have you thought about organising a Family Learning Day, as advocated by the Campaign for Learning? Schools that have done so report impressive and enjoyable occasions, with everything from self-defence to cookery, from beginners' Spanish to folk music being offered. Tutors are anyone on the staff (see Chapter 4) and one school reported the pleasure of the catering assistants in being freed from some of the shackles of school menus in offering exciting and healthy fare of their own design. The day also offered parents and children the chance to eat together!

References

Beresford, E. and Hardie, A. (1996) 'Parents and secondary schools: a different approach' in J. Bastiani and S. Wolfendale (eds) *Home-School Work in Britain*. London: David Fulton.

Briggs, A. (2001) 'Managing the learning environment' in D. Middlewood and N. Burton (eds) *Managing the Curriculum*. London: Paul Chapman.

Coleman, P. (1998) *Parent, Student and Teacher Collaboration: The Power of 3*. London: Paul Chapman.

Desforges, C. with Abonchaat, A. (2003) *The Impact of Parental Involvement, Parental Support and Family Education on Pupil Achievement and Adjustment: A Literature Review*. London: DfES.

EOC (2003) *Gender and Poverty in Britain*. Manchester: Equal Opportunities Commission.

Lucas, B. and Smith, A. (2004) *Help Your Child to Succeed Toolkit*. Stafford: Network Educational Press.

Meighan, W. (2001) 'The education of those children taught at home', *Topic*, 23, pp. 38–46, Slough: National Federation for Educational Research.

Middlewood, D. (1999) 'Managing relationships between schools and parents' in J. Lumby and N. Foskett (eds) *Managing External Relations in Schools and Colleges*. London: Paul Chapman.

OECD (1997) *Parents as Partners in Schooling*. Paris: OECD.

Chapter 12

Moving Beyond Conventional Schooling

Preview

This chapter summarises and proposes:

- Four agendas for change which are needed
  1. A new strategic direction.
  2. A new approach to teaching and learning.
  3. A new perspective on community education.
  4. Building schools for the future.
- The implications of these changes for stakeholders of learning schools.

> *When the challenge is greatest the reform must be boldest.*
>
> Tony Blair

Four agendas for change

1. A new strategic direction

Fullan (2003 p.22) comments:

> *The biggest problem facing schools is fragmentation and overload. It is worse for schools than for business firms. Both are facing uncertain environments, but only schools are suffering the additional burden of having a torrent of unwanted, unco-ordinated policies and innovations raining down on them from hierarchical bureaucracies.*

If we agree with this – and we do – then the case for a new strategic direction is eloquently made. A recurrent theme running through this book has been, perhaps unsurprisingly, that we have now entered an era in education where:

- incremental change will no longer be good enough;
- the next generation of learners will need many more personalised and targeted opportunities if they are to be equipped to deal with the complexities of a millennium which will see accelerated change;

- demands will be placed on an emerging workforce unlike anything that has gone before.

If we are going to be successful in developing an education fit for the twenty-first century, all the stakeholders have got to be prepared to work in partnership. Although such sentiments may seem obvious, all the evidence to date shows that attempts to put in place planned programmes aimed at improving or developing existing practice have met with a variety of mixed responses which have in turn frustrated those entrusted with the task of leading initiatives and more often than not left them powerless and disillusioned.

> *The dilemma for well-intentioned governments is considerable. If they trust local entities to take policies seriously, to take advantage of resources, only a few will systematically do so. If they force the issue by increasing accountability, they foster cultures of superficial dependence.*
>
> (Fullan, 2001 p. 225)

A good example at the time of writing is the ongoing debate in the UK about how best to divide the calendar year up in order to ensure that the most effective learning takes place. The government has looked at four-, five- and six-term year patterns and appears persuaded by the latter model. Although the dispassionate observer will immediately see the merits of the proposed change, not least the timing of examinations and the fact that students applying to higher education will already know their results, the proposal has already created deep divisions, as a report in a recent newsletter makes clear:

> *The change, which would mean the abolition of the traditional six-week summer break as a fixture in the school year, is opposed by many teachers and has sparked talk of industrial action. The NASUWT has insisted that it is 'steadfastly opposed' to alterations to term dates and would consider strike action if individual councils introduced the proposed change unilaterally.*

The significance of this impasse is less to do with the merits of the proposal and more to do with the extent to which those involved are really putting learning at the centre of their arguments. All too often objections to proposed change are based on an approach that regards all change with suspicion and defends the status quo primarily because it *is* the status quo. In the UK there are similar tensions and conflicts about, for example:

- the use of teaching assistants and their place in the learning dynamic;
- the control and management of adult learning in community education programmes;
- the arguments for and against a national funding formula for schools in order to establish transparency and equality;
- the extent to which local education authorities have a strategic role in individual school planning and target setting;

- the most appropriate and effective providers of initial teacher training – schools or higher education?

Although these few examples – and there are countless more – are UK based we are confident that educationalists throughout the world would be able to identify with them and add extensively to the list. At a London conference in June 2002 to launch a major new initiative – the setting up of the Innovation Unit, a government task force designed to seek out and disseminate nationally new approaches to teaching and learning – the Prime Minister confessed his real frustration at not being able to get what he recognised as a great idea from the centre into the field of operation in the same form as it was presented to him. By the time it had passed through several layers of bureaucracy and even more layers of political interpretation it had changed out of all recognition. If we are to have any hope whatsoever of introducing the level and complexity of change needed for new learning schools to be effective this fundamental problem will have to be addressed.

The guiding principle for all those charged with the task of providing effective learning must be to put the needs of the learners first. The shift in importance in the educational system needs to be as shown in Figure 12.1.

In reversing the traditional hierarchy in this way the politicians in the New Republic of South Africa revisited the role and purpose of decision makers. Hargreaves (2003 p.164) expands on this thinking:

> As governments, teachers and citizens, our task is to create a visionary social movement that will provide opportunity for the weak, safety and security for

Figure 12.1 *From national top-down to bottom-up (adapted).*

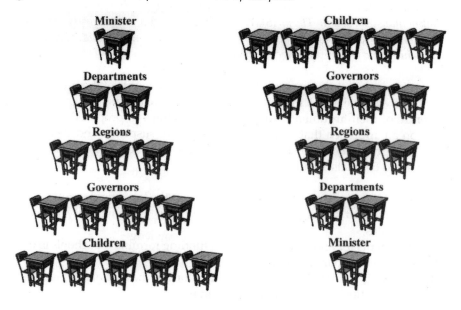

everyone and community for all of us in a more dynamic and inclusive society that harnesses the collective intelligence of all its people, and cultivates the social capital and cosmopolitan identity that will enable people to live and work together.

Political propaganda, local power struggles, individual egos, self-interested electioneering – all need to give way to a corporate will to sacrifice personal agendas and work together for what is perceived as the general good to find strategies to manage the level and complexity of change demanded by this new information-rich age.

2. A new approach to teaching and learning

Throughout this book, we have emphasised the need to make learning rather than teaching the primary aim of education. Whereas in the previous century such an objective may have been seen as sensible and honourable, now it is an imperative: if students do not develop independent learning skills from the outset, they will not be able to cope with the complexities of the twenty-first century. The UK's School Standards minister (Miliband, 2004) wrote in a pamphlet to the Specialists Schools Trust:

> *A new generation of self-confident, independent students is, of course, a challenge. But it is also a genuine opportunity significantly to raise the productivity of the education system – by tailoring teaching and learning to individual need, and developing students as more active partners in effective learning.*

He used the term 'personalised learning' (discussed in earlier chapters) to describe what he envisaged as tailoring teaching and learning to individual need. The concept of personalised learning must be educationally sound – after all we would all sign up to an educational system which ensured that all learners, regardless of age, background or ability reached their full potential.

The significance of this fundamental shift of emphasis is huge, raising as it does any number of tough questions. For example:

- How can we organise and manage national educational systems to cater for individual learners' needs?
- How can we measure success in publicly accountable terms for a generation of learners who will be developing at different rates?
- Do we, in fact, need public certification of success?
- How will e-learning be deployed and utilised to best effect to target personalised learners' needs?
- Will we be able to create a twenty-first century curriculum which will foster the critical thinking skills for the knowledge society in which we now live?
- How will we develop in our students the acknowledgement that rewards can be intrinsic and learning can be valuable for its own sake?

These are only a few of the many questions that arise when we begin to explore the notion of schools as learning organisations.

Taking greater responsibility

In response to the retort that surely schools, by definition, are learning organisations, Clarke (2000 p.20) disagrees:

> *Schools are still modelled on modern structures which assume hierarchical, sequential, linear and technical understandings of learning which promote instruction and efficiency and excellence but within a context that will inevitably fail.*

Clarke sees learning schools 'as places of choice, places of security where it is OK to dream'. He also believes that they will be places geared to nurturing individual qualities:

> *There will need to be opportunities for learners, both teachers and students, to make relevant choices and decisions in their own learning, and this has to be responsive rather than predetermined.*

(ibid p.21)

We consider that the requirement for learning to be **responsive** rather that **predetermined** is crucially important. Fullan (2001 p.17) describes learning organisations as 'energy and knowledge creators'. That creativity comes from being responsive and proactive – key factors in positive learning. Allied to this is a requirement for students to take greater responsibility for their own learning.

Case example one

A large mixed comprehensive school in Nottingham has, for the last three years, been using students to help evaluate the effectiveness of the teaching and learning. This has involved giving teachers informed and systematic feedback on where the strengths and weaknesses were, where they as learners felt involved and where they lost interest, and what strategies the teacher might think of employing in subsequent lessons. Although the teachers were initially extremely dubious about participating in what they knew would be honest and uncluttered student views, the experiment has proved to be a great success. Although the students have on occasions been critical, they have also been extremely complimentary when previously they would have said nothing. The other major plus has been a genuine realisation on the students' part about the contribution they have to make in the learning for it to be truly worthwhile.

Increasing flexibility and choice

It seems highly unlikely that any education system could offer unlimited freedom for each student to follow his or her 'perfect' route. However, if we manage to increase the flexibility of the pathways, it compels the student to exercise choice at every step of the way rather than just at the outset.

Case example two

In the UK, the new draft proposals for 14–19 year-olds are an attempt to increase the flexibility offered to individual learners. By providing a common core and what is termed 'main learning', students have a basic entitlement linked to a curriculum framework which supports specialised learning and allows young people to select programmes to pursue their own interests at their own pace. The underpinning principle guiding this reform is coherence, structure and relevance linked to clear choices for subsequent progression whilst also allowing for learner choice and for movement within different routes. The initial reaction from teachers has been very positive.

Whether or not these reforms improve on the status quo, the significant points to note are how:

- this structure is much more geared to creating space for innovative learning and teaching;
- it encourages choice and diversity;
- learners move at their own pace;
- students do not have to complete each section before moving on because, it is argued, that is not how people learn and work.

E-learning

While we have made passing reference to e-learning in this book the fact remains that it has emerged over the last decade as one of the most powerful tools for revolutionising learning and one of the clearest areas where students can become the teachers and vice versa! It is still a relatively new approach to learning which has only emerged with the recent development of the internet. Evidence to date would suggest that learners do not make decisions unilaterally about whether they access e-learning or more traditional providers. E-learning works most effectively when it is delivered by a combination of online and offline provision. Sensitive, targeted use of e-learning will create opportunities for students to follow a personalised curriculum tailored to their needs by integrating the ever changing face of ICT into education in order to improve teaching and learning.

Case example three

At Chafford Hundred Campus in Thurrock, Essex, they have developed a 'managed learning environment' called The Connetix. The Connetix Learning Environment enables teachers to follow the UK government's ideas of tailored learning for each child. The system allows a whole lesson to be planned and run within the learning environment which can then be tailored to meet the needs of each child. The children's overall performance in the end of year attainment tests (SATS) has improved significantly.

Although the problems associated with the new technologies – currency, reliability, inappropriate use, access, shelf life etc – are well documented elsewhere, there is still overwhelming evidence that new learning schools will have to discover and sustain the ICT expertise within their own organisations to ensure that its potential is harnessed to greatest effect.

The research engaged school

Teachers in new learning schools will need to pursue their own learning.

> *It is vital that teachers engage in action, inquiry and problem-solving together in collegial teams or professional learning communities. Through such teams, teachers can undertake joint curriculum development, respond effectively and creatively to external reform imperatives, engage in collaborative action research, and analyse pupil achievement data together in ways that benefit their pupils' learning.*

> (Hargreaves, 2003 p.17)

Just as hospital consultants need to keep up to date and dentists who fail to do so go out of business, so teachers need to engage in action research which will impact on their own and their respective organisation's practice. Again, Hargreaves (2003 p.20) argues:

> *Teachers who are catalysts of the knowledge society must therefore try to make their schools into learning organisations where capacities to learn and structures that support learning and respond constructively to change are widespread among adults as well as among children.*

Emphasising the need for action research in twenty-first century schools reinforces the importance of constantly questioning and challenging the status quo. Teachers who stop learning themselves prevent others from learning. Relying on certain pedagogical practices because they are familiar rather than effective will not create an environment which encourages learning to be responsive and proactive.

Case example four

In a large comprehensive school in Devon, every member of staff has been asked to produce a piece of research in the form of a 2,000-word report by the end of the Christmas term. These reports will be accredited by the local higher education provider and will count towards a Masters' qualification. The teachers have been given extra time off timetable, thanks to government funding, to complete the research. The finished reports will then be disseminated, discussed in open forum, acted upon as deemed appropriate and then form part of the school's professional development library.

It is, therefore, vital that staff as well as students have access to individual learning opportunities. By so doing, new learning schools will foster a culture of lifelong learning where the acquisition of knowledge will be seen as something embraced by all, not 'done' to some by others.

3. A new perspective on community education

We have made frequent references in previous chapters to the fact that new learning schools will be *in* the community, *for* the community and not in any sense operating in splendid isolation. Clarke (2000 p.27) makes the distinction between 'schooling', where schools are communities of learners, where individuals are helped to reach their potential, and 'learning' where schools are learning communities where everyone is both teacher and learner. If we extend this idea, then it is both natural and sensible to acknowledge the part communities, including business and industry, will play in student and adult learning in twenty-first century schools.

Case example five

The Extended Schools Initiative was launched by the UK government in the White Paper 'A New Specialist System: Transforming Secondary Education' (2003). Extended Schools will create wider partnerships by offering services and facilities at the hub of their communities which will benefit students, their families and other people as well as revitalising neighbourhoods by creating opportunities for lifelong learning.

Extending the range and client market in this way significantly alters the way in which schools operate. For example:

- the concept of 'compulsory schooling' becomes subsumed into a culture of life-long learning;

- by entering into partnerships with a wide range of service providers, schools become 'one stop shops' for their respective communities;
- offering adult classes – including access to higher education and training – blurs the traditional divisions between discrete educational sectors;
- in developing sophisticated strategies for deploying the new technologies, schools will be able to target a much wider audience 24 hours a day and in so doing fundamentally change the way people learn;
- teachers' roles in Extended Schools will expand and diversify. Individually negotiated contracts will become the norm. Long established school hours with built in organisation-wide holiday patterns will quickly become a thing of the past.

These are only a few of the potential developments, but the more you explore the concept of schools extending their current spheres of influence, the greater their potential for revolutionising learning.

Case example six

A large multi-cultural comprehensive in central England is already, with its 2,000+ students, adult learning centre and early years provision, well on the way to becoming an Extended School. It has recently built a state of the art sports centre which will now be used not just for delivering the formal curriculum but also for community health related fitness programmes. For example, all students who are transferring to the school in the coming academic year will, along with their parents, have a full fitness assessment undertaken by trained physical education staff at the school. They will then be recommended to follow tailor-made out of hours fitness programmes in the sports hall run by the school in partnership with the local health centre.

What is particularly exciting about developments such as this is the obvious potential for expansion and innovation. We can only scratch the surface in this book, but we are confident that the community dimension in new learning schools will, over the next few decades, be a prime driver for radical change.

4. Building schools for the future

There is, therefore, overwhelming evidence that schools in the twenty-first century will operate in wholly new ways. There is also much to suggest that they will also look very different. Certainly, the current designs being put forward for the UK's city academies initiative by international architects of the stature of Sir Norman Foster are poles apart from the familiar conventional hall/corridors/classrooms/school hall model of the last two centuries. The new generation of school buildings have entrances that look more like shopping malls. They have restaurants, not dining halls, and ICT in every accessible communal space. Some have dispensed with staffrooms and one recently built business and enterprise specialist college even has its own stock exchange! This new freedom has encouraged those school leaders fortunate enough to have the necessary capital to build a new school or significantly modify an existing one to dispense with conventional wisdoms and put learning rather than structures at the heart of their designs.

We know of one school where the library was far too small for the number of students. The school next door was being completely rebuilt. The solution was to change the library into an Inclusion Centre for children with learning difficulties and redesign the other school's now defunct sports hall into a learning centre complete with twenty-first century library for the use of the three schools on the extended campus and for the local community.

We have already cited in another chapter examples of innovative capital projects already up and running; however, the following two case studies illustrate the potential for radical free thinking.

Case example seven

The Australian Science and Mathematics School (ASMS) has been built to implement leading edge developments in secondary education from the ground up. It has been designed with maximum flexibility and adaptability to promote the concept that teaching may occur at any time, in any place, in many ways, supported by what they describe as 'an ubiquitous ICT-rich environment'. There are no classrooms; instead there are 'learning commons' and 'studios' which allow students to work independently or in groups ranging from two to 200. Social facilities blend closely with formal study areas and the 'school day' is sufficiently flexible to allow students, all of whom have individual learning plans, to move through a range of areas in the building depending on their specific needs at the time.

The ASMS is only one of literally thousands of new approaches to school design. The significance of these developments cannot, in our view, be over-estimated. For the first time in education, there is a clear and rapidly growing acknowledgement that 'conventional schooling' will not meet current and anticipated demands. Equally significant is the extent to which 'learning' is no longer seen as a discrete activity. Many schools, like ASMS, are seeing all aspects of development – in particular the soft social skills – as forming an integral part of the learning day. Awareness of the environment is also high on the list of priorities, as the following example exemplifies.

Case example eight
A recently built primary school in North West England features an energy saving, intelligent building management system which controls ventilation, heating and lighting plus a rainwater recycling facility. There is also a natural fresh air ventilation system, maintenance free timber framing and cladding and sustainable natural drainage. As well as saving costs and energy, it is intended that the school's environmental credentials will be used as an educational tool.

In its pamphlet *Building Schools for the Future* (2003), the UK's Department for Education and Skills made the following statement:

We are moving into a world where every school will have an area of the curriculum specialism and excellence at its heart and throughout all its activity; where every school will be engaged in local collaborations to improve the professional development of teachers and support staff, as well as providing new and exciting opportunities for young people; where ICT will be integral to teaching and learning, not a bolt-on; where community and out of hours teaching and learning will become a more important part of everyday school life, with some facilities being shared between pupils and teachers in neighbouring schools; where first class working environments will be a reality for all teachers and support staff; and where partnerships with other parts of the education system will be the norm and will tailor education to fulfil the needs and aspirations of individual pupils.

This seems to us to be an eloquent summary not just of the arguments put forward in this chapter but also an accurate reflection of much of what has been discussed throughout the book. It is now the responsibility of all those with a vested interest in creating educational life chances for every member of the local and wider community to make the rhetoric become a reality.

Implications

You may be reading this book as a current or future teacher, parent, principal, governor, assistant, community worker or whatever. As some or all of the changes and developments described in this chapter and indeed the whole book take place, we can be certain of at least two things:

- that these roles will evolve;
- that schools will continue to involve even greater numbers of stakeholders and therefore that new roles will emerge.

In this final section of the book therefore, it may be interesting to reflect on what form these roles may be taking in the future and how they differ from today. We believe they all offer exciting and fulfilling possibilities for those of you doing these jobs.

Teacher

Your pattern of working will be different. You may be working in a school with a continuous learning day, so your breaks will be at various times. The pattern of terms and years will be different. You may come in to work early, leave early afternoon and return in the evening. You will have the chance to negotiate an individual employment contract, to be modified as your domestic needs alter:

- You will not be expected to be a fount of all knowledge and will not feel guilty or embarrassed because your students know more than you do in some areas, especially ICT.
- There will be lots of other people having inputs into and influence on students' learning. At times, you may find this frustrating but you remain the key professional, guiding and co-ordinating these inputs.
- Above all, your status as a teacher will rise and rise and, partly because there may be fewer of you, your pay will rise also!
- Your opportunities to develop yourself will be respected, and supported, and your achievement applauded.

Parent

- Since schools will be much more flexible organisations, your own domestic and working habits may be challenged. However, you will find the school more accessible to you at times convenient to you. You will receive much more information electronically and will not be made to feel guilty if you are not able to attend the school physically very much.
- You will realise that the school knows that your son or daughter has intelligence, regardless of test scores, and treats them as such.
- You will understand that the best educational support you can give your child is emotional support and security.
- You will become aware that the fun your child has with some activities, e.g. some computer games, is part of his or her learning programme and that head down over a book is not the only 'proper learning'.
- You will know that if you and/or your child has difficulties, there is a whole range of expert support available on site.
- The school recognises that you too are a learner and will support you where it can.
- When you learn together with your child, the school will applaud this and not see you as interfering.

Learning assistant

- As a para-professional, your job will be seen as crucial in working alongside teachers and a range of other staff to support student learning. Neither the student nor parent will be focusing attention on the specifics of people's roles, their focus will be on the learning.

- Within the school, you will be part of one staff with common facilities and opportunities.
- You will not be seen as a 'dogsbody' but as one of a team of people.
- You will be a personal tutor for a number of students and receive that tremendous feeling of celebration and achievement when one of 'your' tutees gains an apprenticeship in electronics or a Doctorate in Philosophy.
- You will be expected to make use of your skills and talents and encouraged to continue learning and receive support and recognition for what you achieve.

Headteacher/principal

- You will have less and less time for operational or maintenance issues. You will need to be updating the school's vision constantly to check that it is able to adjust to the ever changing social, political and environmental issues that will arise.
- You will need to develop ways in which you have a sense of what people are feeling and thinking about the school as a place of learning. You will still be seen as the prime person for being accountable.
- You will spend very little time on detailed analysis of test or exam results and more on ways in which you can assess whether individuals' learning is progressing – much more difficult but much less boring than results analysis precisely because it is about individuals.
- People will look to you as the person to try to influence national or regional policy.
- You will be seen as a key person in the community, one who helps give moral and emotional leadership and guidance and your key decisions will be judged according to the impact they may have on a much wider constituency than at present.
- You will have more time to engage with some individual learners, including those who exist in challenging circumstances.
- You will be expected to be a role model for personal learning, partly under the public gaze. Its advantage, among others, is that when you do retire, that part of your life continues seamlessly.

Middle leaders

- Your role will have little emphasis on organisational issues. You will not be managing systems for groups of people.
- Rather, you will be focused on having responsibility for the learning of a whole range of people, children and adults.
- Yours will be a role with essentially a co-ordinating emphasis, with a responsibility for monitoring the effectiveness of that learning. You will be using, above all, people skills to encourage, motivate, challenge and inspire learners.

- Your own learning and development will be encouraged and supported. You will be expected to set an example.

Governor

- Your main role will be in seeing yourself as an active link between the school and its community. You belong to that community and it is your job to keep the school and your fellow governors up to date with the community's needs and changes.
- You will need to remind yourself constantly that children's learning is what the school and therefore you exist for. All 'your' children are intelligent in their different ways.
- You will be expected to do a radical audit every so often, enabling you to resist the view that because something has worked alright in the past, it must be good for the future.
- This audit will enable you to change the use of your resources to make best use of them.
- You will not waste valuable time comparing your school with others.
- You will demonstrate your commitment to learning by being a role model for personal learning.

And finally, the student

- You will find yourself working harder, but smarter. It will be more challenging but not in a dreary, slogging, 'let's keep at it' way. You will have to take responsibility for decisions about your own learning e.g. deciding what to opt for, agreeing with others when you feel ready to take an assessment.
- You will learn to admit your mistakes and see them as things to learn from.
- You will be less dependent upon your teacher but aware that a whole range of people exist to help you and, in many cases, learn with you.
- What you learn out of school will be very closely linked with and seen as part of what you learn at school.
- You will have opportunities to influence how your school develops, how your teachers operate, how your work is assessed.
- You will be less concerned with test and exam results and especially with what other people achieved.
- You will recognise the kind of intelligent person you are and that your individual needs really do count.
- When things are difficult, your school will be there to help you, along with a whole range of other support services.
- You will come to know that learning is enjoyable and you will not be able to stop!

References

Clarke, P. (2000) *Learning Schools, Learning Systems*. London: Continuum.

Department for Education and Skills (2003) *Building Schools for the Future*. London: DfES.

Fullan, M. (2001) *The New Meaning of Educational Change*. London: RoutledgeFalmer.

Hargreaves, A. (2003) *Teaching in the Knowledge Society*. Buckingham: Open University.

Miliband, D. (2004) *Personalised Learning: The Route to Excellence and Equity*. Specialist Schools Trust.

Glossary

GLOSSARY OF TERMS USED

ASMS	Australian Science and Mathematics School.
AST	Advanced Skills Teacher.
BBC	British Broadcasting Corporation.
CATS	Cognitive Ability Tests.
DfES	Department for Education and Skills.
EOC	Equal Opportunities Commission.
EQ	Emotional Quotient.
FE	Further Education
GCSE	General Certificate of Secondary Education.
HE	Higher Education.
ICT	Information and Communications Technology.
INSET	In-service Education and Training.
IQ	Intelligence Quotient.
KS	Key Stage.
LEA	Local Education Authority.
MI	Multiple Intelligences.
MIDYIS	Mid-years Information Systems.
MRI	Magnetic Resonance Imaging.
NASUWT	National Association of Schoolmasters and Union of Women Teachers.
NCSL	National College for School Leadership.
NLP	Neuro-Linguistic Programming.
OECD	Organisation for Economic and Cultural Development.
OFSTED	Office for Standards in Education.
PSHE	Personal, Social and Health Education.
QCA	Qualifications and Curriculum Authority.
RSA	Royal Society for the Arts.
TES	*Times Education Supplement.*
VAK	Visual, Auditory, Kinaesthetic.
WIIFM	What's in it for me?
YELLIS	Year Eleven Information Systems.

Index